THE WEAPONS MERCHANTS

Also by Bernt Engelmann

MEINE FREUNDE DIE MILLIONÄRE
DAS EIGENE NEST
DEUTSCHLAND REPORT
MEINE FREUNDE DIE MANAGER
EINGANG NUR FÜR HERRSCHAFTEN

BERNT ENGELMANN

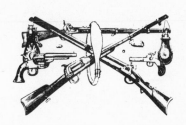

THE WEAPONS MERCHANTS

translated from the German by
ERICA DETTO

CROWN PUBLISHERS, INC., NEW YORK

CONTENTS

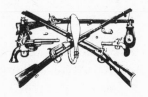

BUSINESS
WITH DEATH

IT IS DIFFICULT to imagine a person's feelings when he discovers after a twelve-hour journey over rough terrain in a pickup truck with extremely poor shock absorbers that the uncomfortable seat he has been traveling on is in fact a crate containing loosely packed land mines.

I could feel my back hair standing on end, and as soon as I had regained my composure, I did not hesitate to voice my exasperation. I told Omar the driver loud and clear what I thought of him and his carelessness. I also expressed my determination to walk the rest of the way. "Then at least *I* will arrive in one piece," I concluded.

"Inschallah!" replied Omar, and grinned. "If it is the Lord's will!"

To reach our destination we had to travel about another twenty miles. Dusk was falling but we would get there before dark, by car. On foot, without light, through unknown rugged terrain, passing nervous guards and trigger-happy patrols, my arrival would be extremely uncertain. After giving the matter considerable thought, I decided on the land mines as the lesser evil, and continued with Omar.

7

The journey, which ended an hour later in front of a log cabin near the Algeria-Tunisia border, was my first direct contact with the big business on the edge of the little wars.

The mines I had so innocently traveled on came from Europe and were bound for the ALN (*Armée de Libération Nationale*), the national Algerian liberation army, and their war against French rule in North Africa. I had accompanied them on the next-to-last stretch; the last link of the transportation chain led through the near-impenetrable blockade system of the Maurice Line directly to the Algerian guerrillas, who intended to disrupt the supply and connection lines of their far superior enemies.

Who were the mine suppliers? What price had been paid? And how were they smuggled to the North African war zone from a country possibly friendly and allied with France?

These questions occupied my thoughts more than my assignment, which was to write a special report about the military strength of the Algerian Liberation Movement.

The more I saw of the Algerian war, the more these questions persisted.

The long-moustached guard in front of the log cabin wore an American combat suit, a brand-new German Mauser carbine 98K, which, as I very well knew, no longer was manufactured in Germany, and on his belt a bowie knife, no doubt inscribed "Made in Solingen, Germany," of the type preferred by the Hitler-youth movement of the Third Reich.

A young officer, a reddish-blond Berber, greeted me politely, and against all commandments imposed by the Prophet Mohammed emptied a glass of red wine with me. He was armed with an Italian Beretta. The NCO, whose bed I should occupy for the night, put at my disposal a German Army canteen, American cigarettes, a French Army water bottle, and a Czech automatic pistol—for emergencies, he said.

The next morning I saw German antiaircraft guns, mortars, and bazookas, British and American rifles, and two field howitzers of Swiss origin. I had lunch with the man responsible for supplying all this war matériel, Si Abd-el-Hafid Bussuf, Minister for Supply and Logistics of the then Algerian Government-in-Exile. The French Government in Algeria had put an enormous price on his head.

Over a tasty risotto from the field kitchen we talked about many things until I plucked up the courage to ask him for a few details about the "ammunition crate," not his trade secrets, of course, but perhaps his personal impressions of those who sold him weapons. These were men who sold pistols and explosives as uninhibitedly as others sell vacuum cleaners or soap.

Men in the shadow:
secret meeting of the Algerian Liberation Front. On the left, Si Abd-el-Hafid Bussuf, Logistics and Communications Chief; on the right, Commander in Chief Bel Cacem Krim.

Photo: Karl Breyer, Bad Aachen

An outstanding customer:
Bernt Engelmann discussing the market with Bel Cacem Krim, commander of the Algerian guerrillas (ALN).

Photo: Petra Engelmann, Hamburg

"You know," Bussuf said smilingly, "weapons dealers are an indispensable part of a revolution. In their own way they serve the progress of humanity. What would have become of the American Declaration of Independence without General Washington's business connections with some efficient weapons dealers? Moreover," Bussuf continued, "weapons dealers are merchants just like others. They take risks to make profits, and they are trying to establish a sensible relationship between risk and profit. Some are honest merchants, while others are swindlers; just common business practices, you know. And they are really not so daring and romantic as most people imagine."

Despite Bussuf's warnings, my interest had been aroused, and I have since found the weapons merchants a fascinating group. Whether this opinion is justified may be decided by the reader. I shall, in the following chapters of this book, introduce a number of men and women whose business with death is nothing extraordinary, just routine. The reader will meet them as I met them.

A MAN
FROM TANGIER

I SHOULD BE USED TO FLYING because of the distances I have traveled, both in tiny, ancient one-engine aircraft and in gigantic supermodern jetliners. However, whenever I board an airplane I become frightened, and curse myself and a profession that takes me to all corners of the world.

On March 3, 1959, about 9:15 P.M., I was on the regular flight from Tunis to Frankfurt. The airliner, a comfortable, safe bird with only well-behaved people on board and a first-class efficient pilot at the controls, performed the prescribed landing pattern. The Frankfurt airport lights shone reassuringly through the rain clouds. I clung frantically to my seat, closed my eyes, and concentrated on whether I would make my connections and reach home in about two hours, or whether the customs officials would comment unfavorably on my voluminous ration of cigarettes and whiskey, and then, because they are generally courteous people, ignore it. Ten minutes later, after a perfect landing, I was again in the best of spirits: I was on solid ground; the customs officials had been lenient; and my connecting flights were assured.

I saw myself arriving home.

But then my name was called over the public address system: ". . . please come to the information desk." Expecting the worst, I made my way there and received the following telegram, which had just arrived: "Interrupt return trip for further investigations—Trade Fair visitor Georg Puchert from Tangier, Morocco, victim of bomb explosion. No clues. Suspect political motives related to North Africa."

I sighed. . . .

My hope that I would be home in two hours was destroyed, and I already foresaw difficulties. I would have to rely mainly on information released by the police. As I well knew, the meager stream of information from the Homicide Squad would soon slow to a trickle if the motivation for a crime could not be determined within the usual criminal ranges but led instead into the entanglement of political intrigue—a horror to criminal investigators. Furthermore, the Trade Fair in Frankfurt had just begun, and the thousands of German and foreign visitors presented numerous additional difficulties. I would not, for example, find hotel accommodations. Newspapers think of a good many things, but one important aspect they always neglect is to secure hotel rooms for their reporters.

After returning from a long stay in Africa, the prospect of spending the first night in Germany in a railway station waiting room was so unattractive that I decided to ignore the telegram. My flight to Hamburg would leave in ten minutes, and my luggage was on board. But just at that moment I happened to see the front-page headline of next morning's newspaper: "Bomb explosion in Frankfurt's West End." Below the picture of a torn-up Mercedes was the next line in large block letters: "Body riddled with steel pellets."

Where had I seen a very similar picture recently?

While the noisy traffic of the busy airport continued to mill around me, I tried to remember; and suddenly I knew: Three months earlier, in Rabat, the Moroccan capital, a European had died in the same manner when a bomb exploded under his car in the heart of the city—but I had forgotten the victim's name. Bombings in North Africa were no rarity, but I had given

At the head of the Red Hand's blacklist:
Georg Puchert, alias Captain Morris.

special attention to that case because I had just spent some time in Rabat, and today's bombing now reminded me of a similar crime committed in Germany.

In Hamburg, in the summer of 1957, a Mercedes disintegrated in a bomb explosion in the middle of town at high noon. A woman died, but the man on whose life the attempt was made escaped unhurt. His name was Otto Schlüter, a Hamburg resident and the owner of a sporting-goods store specializing in hunting weapons.

Three auto bombings in three cities! Three dead, one of the victims a European in Morocco.

Today's Frankfurt victim, Georg Puchert, also came from Tangier. And as I remembered, the man from Hamburg, Otto Schlüter, allegedly had business connections with Morocco—dealings in weapons, as reported in all the newspapers at that time. Because of the remarkable parallels, I toyed with the idea of remaining in Frankfurt. But the thought of spending the night in the railway station was enough to dissuade me; and then another announcement came through the loudspeaker: "Because of weather conditions, Lufthansa regrets to announce cancellation of the flights to Düsseldorf, Cologne, and Hamburg. Will all passengers concerned please go to the airline counters?"

Decisions, it seems, are made elsewhere; consequently, my concern about decent quarters for the night became somebody else's problem.

One hour later I began an investigation, never suspecting that it would extend over many years, and three continents.

Newspaper reporters encounter more obstacles than the police. No one is compelled to answer reporters' bothersome questions; they cannot summon people, interrogate them, confront or arrest them. They have no identification department or criminal records at their disposal, no access to files, reports or experts' opinions. But sometimes newspaper reporters have an advantage over the police. Because they have no legal power and cannot interrogate, search, or arrest people, they are permitted where a police officer without a search warrant would never be admitted, and sometimes they hear stories that are certainly not meant for police ears. It all depends on circumstances.

During the night of March 3, 1959, circumstances were extremely favorable for me. I began my investigation in such comfortable surroundings, and so successfully, as to make any investigator green with envy.

In the event of unforeseen delays, airlines provide excellent accommodations in luxury hotels for their passengers. One can meet some very interesting people in such places. This night I could even expect to meet some friends or acquaintances, because the Trade Fair was in full swing.

I drank my first whiskey and soda alone at the bar. Around me, lively conversations were under way about the weather, the fair, and, of course, the bombing. I heard that Georg Puchert had frequented this bar, that he was a quiet, friendly man, a moderate drinker. So said the bartender. I also learned that Puchert was accompanied occasionally by his pretty seventeen-year-old daughter and that father and daughter had lived with friends at Lindenstrasse 3. This information was provided by an elegantly dressed middle-aged gentleman sipping French cognac. The bartender's assistant, busying himself with polishing glasses, also made some comments, but was discreetly reprimanded by the bartender for interrupting. Finally, I heard that Georg Puchert had conducted business transactions with a regular patron of the bar, a Norwegian, who was a representative for explosives manufacturers. I listened carefully, but the conversation changed to another subject. Puchert and his acquaintances were forgotten.

I had my second whiskey and soda with another acquaintance who had suddenly appeared beside me, the Economics Attaché to the Arabian Embassy in Bonn. I joked with him for drinking alcohol, considering he was a Moslem, and asked if the Koran provided an exception for visitors to the Frankfurt Trade

Fair. He replied happily that one has to respect the customs of a foreign country; he considered this a matter of the utmost importance. And besides, the Prophet Mohammed did not know about whiskey and soda.

Generally, my acquaintance seemed very relaxed and talkative, until I mentioned the bombing. He was suddenly serious. "This is very bad," he said in a low voice. "The death of Captain Morris is a dreadful blow for the Mudjahidin of Wilaya 5." With a significant glance he hurriedly excused himself—he had to attend to urgent business.

I had heard enough to make me very curious: Mudjahidin were soldiers of the holy war, and this could only mean the rebels of the Algerian uprising. My assumption was confirmed by the Arabian's remark: ". . . a dreadful blow to Wilaya 5." Wilaya were the sections of the Algerian front line; Number 5 was the western section of the Moroccan border.

Gradually, I figured out Puchert's place in the puzzle, but the young attaché did not mention Puchert, but Captain Morris. Was he the same person? Was one of these a pseudonym? In any case, I had made remarkable progress without any effort. I felt I deserved a third, and last, whiskey and soda.

My drink arrived, together with a gentleman who had flown with me from Tunis to Frankfurt. He was a man of comfortable means, a middle-aged Dutchman with apple-pink cheeks and graying temples. He spoke excellent German, and told me that he had suffered the same fate—his flight had been canceled and he was staying at the same hotel.

We enjoyed a relaxed conversation about the weather; it was so much colder here than in North Africa. I mentioned that only yesterday I had been on La Marsa beach, sunbathing. He told me that he had been skiing a few days in the snow in Ifran. I happened to know this small Moroccan town in the Central Atlas Mountains. Oddly enough, it resembled a health resort in the Black Forest. I had an idea. "Are you familiar with the area there?" I asked. He laughed. "I have been living in Tangier for several years," he said, smiling radiantly, and added that he was the director of a foreign bank there. He introduced himself, and looked at me expectantly. Now it was my turn. I hesitated a few seconds, took a deep breath, introduced myself, and divulged my profession and mission.

"So, he was finally caught, Captain Morris," was his unexpected comment. He sipped his drink slowly, as if saluting a dead friend. I watched him intently. It was obvious that he had known Georg Puchert and that he must also know something about him. Only a limited number of West European, German-speaking businessmen lived in Tangier, and they were bound to meet from time to time. There were two possibilities—my acquaintance would shut up like a clam or he would become talkative. He chose the latter.

I still cannot quite believe my luck, but circumstances were working for me: My Dutch friend and I were traveling together, we both had been delayed, and stayed in the same hotel. The congenial atmosphere in the bar, the whiskey, and the sensational assassination of someone my companion was acquainted with were more than enough to turn a taciturn bank director into a lively source of breathtaking information.

When we parted early in the morning, my head was buzzing with names, dates, and events. One of my main work principles is never to take notes during a conversation. Even the most willing informer will immediately clam up if his words are being put down on paper. I tried to remember all I had heard that night, and wrote it down. The new morning dawned by the time I finished. I opened the window and inhaled the fresh air. The bus to the airport was parked at the hotel entrance. My friend boarded it—and traveled on.

I went to bed, dead tired. Perhaps this was the bed Georg Puchert had slept in the first night of his last trip to Germany, from May 19 to 20, 1958.

This is Georg Puchert's story up to his return to Germany on May 19, 1958, as told to me by my Dutch friend and as confirmed and completed later by several other informed sources.

The Puchert family home was the Latvian port of Libau on the Baltic Sea. They were of German descent, a middle-class family of merchants and shipowners. In 1939–1940 the Baltic countries were invaded and "united" with the Soviet Union, and the Pucherts escaped to Germany. Georg, then in his mid-twenties, joined the German Navy. After Germany's collapse he was stranded in Hamburg. He planned to establish a forwarding agency. The necessary capital could be raised if he kept his eyes open. The black market of a major port offered plenty of opportunity. But in spring of 1949 Puchert changed his mind and residence, and steered toward Tangier—at that time an international port free from customs duties and taxes, without control of foreign currency or trade, and a paradise for tough men determined to get rich.

Puchert's wife and children remained in Germany, along with a large sum of worthless "old" money, earned in the black market.

Three final, important steps followed: divorce, currency reform (new money), immigration.

Now Puchert was set on a new start, and he was well equipped for it—he brought a seaworthy cutter, a new wife (a cousin from Libau bearing the same family name), and a baby daughter, who bore the befitting name of Marina, true to the seafaring tradition of her parents. In addition to an oceangoing cutter, Puchert's capital for his new business consisted mainly of his physical strength. These proved to be necessary, because life for the Pucherts in Tangier, or rather *off* Tangier, was not easy. Tangier's international police refused them a residence permit. Two French police inspectors in particular, with whom Puchert had some disagreement, were determined to prevent their landing.

Bearing the humiliation and without a permanent dwelling, the Pucherts lived on their cutter for three years. Then, through Latvian friends in London, Puchert's wife obtained a new passport. Finally they could reside on land.

During this long waiting period Georg Puchert had not been idle. Exemption from customs duties, owning an ocean-

going cutter, and having strong shoulders were a useful combina-
tion. Utilizing all these, he made progress in Tangier, even without a permanent address on dry land. Smuggling cigarettes to
Spain, Malta, and especially Italy, Puchert accumulated a small
fortune, and also acquired the nickname "Captain Morris" after
his favorite cigarettes, a name that soon earned him respect
and a reputation in related circles of the western Mediterranean.
With his increasing wealth he legalized and expanded his enterprise. After all, smuggling tobacco, though illegal, was not dis-
honorable, nor were the laws prohibiting it strictly enforced.
In fact, smuggling such innocent merchandise was socially ac-
ceptable, and one of the pillars of Tangier's flourishing economy.
Puchert, however, lacked a captain's license and official documents for his ship—serious deficiencies even on these tolerant
shores. He bought a captain's license for $1,000 from a re-
spected businessman who was representing the Central American republic of Costa Rica.

Gradually Puchert acquired a flotilla of cutters. All his
boats carried romantic names, and were recorded in the ships'
register at Puerto Limón, a desolate place on Costa Rica's Ca-
ribbean coast, a port they had never seen.

Flying the proud blue, white, and red flag of the midget
coffee republic, under the heavy hand of Captain Morris, the
Bruja Roja (Red Witch), the *Wild Dove*, the *Sirocco*, the
Typhoon, and the *Fleur-de-Lis* sailed the western Mediterranean
and the Atlantic, down to the Gulf of Guinea during the early
fifties. Officially they pursued the succulent lobsters in these
waters; but much more lucrative was their unofficial but nevertheless benevolently tolerated smuggling business, which
helped, in a strange way, to realize Puchert's dream of his own
forwarding agency.

The midget flotilla smuggled all sorts of merchandise:
small leather pouches containing raw diamonds from Liberia
for the diamond cutters of Antwerp and Idar-Oberstein (carefully bypassing the London Diamond Syndicate and the European customs authorities, of course), hundreds of thousands
of American cigarettes to puncture the government monopolies

of France, Spain, and Italy, cheap textiles from Hong Kong, cameras and binoculars from Japan, home-distilled "French" cognac, rum from Jamaica, ivory, watches from Switzerland, valuable alloys, eggs from China, and gold ingots.

Smuggling gold was particularly profitable because there were no marketing difficulties, especially in countries with creeping inflation. They would buy any quantity of gold, even paying black-market prices, wherever the valuable metal was available, for instance in Tangier, without restrictions and for only "white" prices.

It was a life of wild adventure, with plenty of ocean, sun, and remuneration, and it was unavoidable that fairly soon a new and dangerous commodity would be added to the wide selection of goods carried by the newly established company. "Astramar" was the company name, and Puchert was the sole owner.

◎

Ever since World War II there had been restlessness in the French-ruled territories of North Africa. In 1953, an armed uprising broke out in Morocco. On November 1, 1954, Algeria erupted in a "National Liberation War," which was to last eight years, while Morocco and Tunisia were to gain independence very much sooner, in 1956.

At the beginning, the chances for Morocco's freedom were slim. There were enough revolution-minded men, but there was a lack of coordination and weapons. Even though the Arabs and Kabyles living in the French and Spanish occupation zones finally established enough unity to take action, the rifles, submachine and machine guns, mortars, and ammunition had to be procured overseas.

Since World War II, such merchandise was abundant. To find dealers willing to sell was no problem. Ready cash was also available. The majority of the rich Moslem merchants from Fez, Marrakech, Rabat, Oujda, Meknes, and Tangier were willing to sacrifice, and the Arab League in Cairo and the oil princes

from the Persian Gulf offered assistance, though not enthusiastically.

The major obstacle, however, was the strict military control exercised by the occupation powers on the borders and
especially in the ports. The obvious approach, therefore, was
to contact the professional blockade runners. Under these circumstances, the Moroccans considered the smugglers of Tangier
a blessing straight from heaven. The daring leaders of the Moroccan uprising figured that among the kaleidoscope of adventurers there was one who would be dependable and prepared to
share in a risky business, a share that would not be entirely
covered and secured by insurance policies.

Such a man was soon found: Georg Puchert, a German
with many years of honorable smuggling experience on the high
seas, not a shady character like a narcotics or white slave trader.
Also, Captain Morris was the owner of several fast cutters that
sailed under a neutral flag. He had a reputation for depend-
ability and discretion and, most important, he had a private
account to settle with two French police inspectors in Tangier.

In the years that followed, Georg Puchert obtained satisfaction in every respect. He took his revenge on the *flics*, the
French police officers—profitably.

Seemingly everything went on as before. His lobster boats
expanded their trips—they sailed to Trieste, Rijeka, Madeira,
and the Canary Islands. The correspondence of Astramar extended all over the world, from Monrovia to Olso, from New
Orleans to Hong Kong. The volume of business increased tremendously, and the organization functioned smoothly. In addition, the new field proved to be very satisfactory. In dark nights
on the high seas Captain Morris's cutters took on board crates
of all sizes and shapes from busy cargo ships, paying cash on
the barrelhead.

Before their return to Tangier, the small boats, without
lights and with their engines cut off, sailed to a quiet little bay
on the Moroccan coast. Brown-skinned men, submerged up to
their necks, were waiting there.

The dangerous cargo was silently unloaded. Minutes later

the cutters took to the sea again. In the darkness the bay was as quiet as before.

Deep in the underbrush along the shore, the crates were loaded on donkeys, and men and beasts departed hurriedly on near-impassable paths leading toward the mountains. The cargo had to reach its destination before daylight.

Even before the *Bruja Roja* or the *Wild Dove* arrived at the Tangier piers, mute young men, at well-protected spots in the mountains, had already assembled the thickly greased parts and put the machine guns and mortars in position.

The French security police soon heard about the activities of Astramar operating out of the Rue Vermeer, where Puchert had recently established his offices. But, officially, not much could be done about this in Tangier's International Zone. The French secret police had to find some method of stopping him.

The rumor was created that Georg Puchert was a Communist, even a top agent, working for the Soviets and assigned the task of destroying the Moroccan Liberation Movement, and that he was an enemy of Islam, the Sultan, and private ownership.

Evidence to support these startling rumors was fabricated, and Puchert's Russian birth was used as a foundation for accusations. His Baltic hometown of Libau was, until 1917, part of the Russian Empire, and then again, in 1940, it was occupied by the Soviets. Other rumors were set off by an intelligence officer who distorted additional facts.

The Moroccans did not believe the accusations because Puchert had always supplied good merchandise, never bad propaganda.

Tangier's European colony quickly discarded the "Communist agent" theory, for Captain Morris was, after all, despite his professional reserve and occasional shrewdness, straightforward and frank. A political agent on a secret mission would act quite differently. Although he was an adventurer, smuggler, and daredevil, Puchert nevertheless conducted his business with honesty, decency, and even with dignity.

True gunrunners, like the profiteers who, from their head-

Multipurpose lobster boats owned by Captain Morris:
on the right, above, *Bruja Roja* (Red Witch) before discovery of her
secret . . .

Photo: Collection Bernt Engelmann

. . . and after.

Photo: Spiegel, Hamburg

quarters at the Hotel Cathay in Shanghai, had kept the Chinese civil war going during the thirties and forties, would have considered Captain Morris naïve. Of course, he dealt in smuggled weapons, and his profits were considerable. But he did not try to capitalize on his situation by continually raising prices, and he did not betray his customers to the police. He did not even double-deal with both parties, a practice common among sellers of weapons. And contrary to the customary practice of seasoned gunrunners, Puchert did not reveal his customers' secrets, and did not even remotely consider selling them to their opponents' intelligence agencies.

Captain Morris was obviously not a typical weapons merchant, and as such was highly valued by his only customer—at the time—the Moroccan Independence Movement. But the French occupation forces in Morocco considered him increasingly more dangerous and undesirable. This attitude was aggravated by the Algerian uprising in 1954.

Puchert's Moroccan friends warmly recommended the capable captain to their Algerian brothers; in 1955 Puchert was the main supplier of the West Algerian guerrillas.

In 1956 Morocco and Tunisia were granted independence, and the Algerian uprising expanded into open war. France tried frantically to hold on to her oldest and most valuable territory in Africa. The measures taken to isolate Algeria and to cut off the supply of weapons to the rebels were ruthless, though understandable from the French viewpoint.

Before long, Puchert felt the effect of these measures. During the summer of 1957, at their Tangier piers, two of his cutters, the *Bruja Roja* and the *Sirocco,* were bombed and destroyed. This was a grave warning, but Captain Morris remained calm. The cutters were replaced; the smuggling of weapons continued; and his ties with Algeria's FLN (*Front de Libération Nationale*) were reinforced; the captain became indispensable to the West Algerian rebels.

Along the Moroccan border the supply situation was desperate. An impenetrable French fortifications system blocked access roads from Morocco. The Moroccan coast was block-

Weapons for Wilaya 5:
mortars from Finland via Hamburg–Casablanca
on the way to the consumer.

Photo: Karl Breyer, Bad Aachen

aded. The overland roads into Tunisia and Libya extended over immense areas, and were again and again bombed and cratered by fighter-bombers.

The West Algerian defense zone, Wilaya 5, bought weapons and ammunition from different sources, and their suppliers took reckless advantage of the emergency situation. Prices spiraled upward.

In May, 1958, a military *coup d'état* overpowered the already weakened Fourth Republic, which was ready to negotiate, sweeping General de Gaulle to the top. The Algerians rightly anticipated a revival of the French fighting spirit, with a subsequent escalation of the war, creating more obstacles for themselves.

About the middle of May, at the Hotel Tour Hassan in Rabat, a war council of the West Algerian rebel leaders hurriedly was assembled, and drastic measures for improving the supply situation in Wilaya 5 were decided upon: immediately to standardize the multitude of weapons and simplify ammunition and spare-parts supplies; build up an Algerian speedboat flotilla to run the blockade off the Moroccan coast; procure large quantities of explosives and prepare a plan to blast open the barriers along the Moroccan-Algerian border and ferry urgently needed supplies through the gaps; and reorganize purchases in Europe by appointing an authorized chief buyer.

The man who was to procure the speedboats and explosives should possess very special qualifications. He should be familiar with the special needs of Wilaya 5, be multilingual, sharp and cunning, capable of playing the gunrunners—who by now acted more and more boldly—against one another and bring down their prices, be able to master the art of logistics, know the market situation in all details, and be experienced with speedboats and North African coastal navigation.

The War Council finally elected Captain Morris for this mission. No one could have been better qualified.

But would he agree?

Puchert did not hesitate. A man without a country, he

For sale:
captured weapons and equipment, bought cheap,
awaiting potential customers.

Photos: Collection Bernt Engelmann

realized his unique chance to obtain power, wealth, and respect in an independent North Africa. But he did not sell himself cheaply. He requested guaranteed citizenship for himself and his family in independent Algeria; staff officer's rank; an appointment as commander of the Algerian Navy, which he was to build up; the supervision of the establishment of a future merchant navy and supervision of all shipyards, docks, and ports; also, for his immediate mission, unlimited powers, and, of course, some financial guaranty for himself and his family.

His conditions were accepted; the compact was solemnly confirmed.

Two days later, on May 19, 1958, Puchert traveled by air via Madrid to Frankfurt. On the evening of his arrival he checked into the same hotel where I would hear his life story—just ten months later, on the day of his death, told by my friend the Dutch banker.

Puchert's plan was, first of all, to contact about two dozen of the more important weapons merchants. Then, as planned, he would play one against the other, bring down their prices, establish more rigid acceptance procedures, and generally put the whole business on a sound basis. And he wanted to purchase the speedboats as soon as possible.

On the morning of May 20, 1958, he continued his trip to Bonn. There he hoped to meet the man on the top of his list of weapons merchants: Hans Joachim Seidenschnur.

Here ends the story of the Dutch banker from Tangier. I never saw him again.

Thinking it over, I realized that my informant must have known Captain Morris fairly well. I was sure that he could have revealed not only the first name on Puchert's list but the others also. Why did he mention only one person? Should I travel to Bonn and visit Seidenschnur?

I decided to wait for a while and to try my luck, first in Frankfurt at Lindenstrasse 3. If the bartender's assistant's information was correct, this had been Puchert's last address.

The house at Lindenstrasse 3 was large, old, and showed traces of war. More than a dozen tenants and many boarders lived there. In which apartment had Captain Morris and his daughter Marina lived?

I climbed the stairs slowly, studied the names on all the doors, but was not too optimistic. On the third floor I stopped, surprised. My search was over. In the dim light of the stair landing I had discovered a sign:

ELS SEIDENSCHNUR
EXCLUSIVE LADIES' FASHIONS

I rang the bell.

The door was opened by a young, strikingly pretty girl dressed in black. She looked at me questioningly.

"Miss Puchert?" I asked cautiously.

She nodded.

What should I say? Slightly confused, I continued, "I arrived here last night, from Tunis. . . ."

She looked at me with large dark eyes. We both heard steps. Somebody came downstairs.

"Please come in," Marina Puchert whispered urgently. "No one should see you!"

She held the door open. I hesitated slightly. The steps came closer. I cursed myself, my ideas, my profession.

I entered the apartment behind Captain Morris's daughter. She closed the door slowly, switched off the light in the hall, and led the way through a pitch-dark corridor to a small drawing room.

Reporters invading the private quarters of the family of a victim assassinated the previous day, for the purpose of interviewing them, naturally arouse distaste—in the bereaved, the public, and, if they are not too unfeeling, themselves. Only the publishers have no objections to such practices.

I felt very uncomfortable, especially since I realized that Marina Puchert did not consider me a snoopy journalist, but a

Captain Morris's soft spot:
daughter Marina.

friend of her father, or perhaps a delegate of the Algerian Government-in-Exile.

I had to do something to get out of this embarrassing situation.

Marina impressed me as being composed and self-confident. But before telling her who I was and what I wanted, I
thought it advisable to secure whatever advantage I had gained
and to soothe my conscience.

Anticipating her first question, I said: "Please, Miss Puchert, before we talk about anything else, I would like to know if
you are in any difficulty. Do you need help? What can I do for
you?"

She replied without hesitation. "We are almost out of
money. . . ."

I did not hesitate. "May I please use the phone?" I asked.

The ambassador in Bonn from one of the African states,
whom I now called, was the most energetic among his colleagues. I had visited him and his country quite often. It was
quite possible that he had known Georg Puchert. I tried: "Ex-
cellency, I am with Miss Marina Puchert. You may have heard
that her father was assassinated yesterday morning. If my information is correct, her father was a special delegate of Wilaya 5.
Marina is without money. Perhaps you want to help."

The reply was brief and positive; I gave him Marina's
address.

That same day, Marina's financial difficulties were over
for the time being—and my guilty conscience was considerably
relieved.

There were still more surprises: A lady entered the room.
She was tall, slender, blonde, cool, good-looking, in her late
thirties. She looked questioningly first at Marina, then at me. "I
did not know you had a visitor. Am I interrupting?"

Marina, suddenly very lively, introduced me to Mrs. Els
Seidenschnur.

"This gentleman comes directly from Tunis," she said.
"He arranged for me to get some money."

The ice was broken.

We talked for hours, like old friends. When I mentioned, incidentally and tactfully, that I was a reporter, it did not bother the ladies.

Late in the afternoon, a messenger came with a considerable sum of money, and when I finally took my leave, I had to promise to return soon. And I had heard the history of Georg Puchert's last ten months.

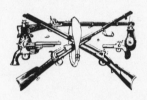

A VISIT
BY PEDRO

ELS SEIDENSCHNUR WAS AN INDEPENDENT BUSINESSWOMAN. In adverse circumstances, she had been forced to become self-supporting, and learned to be an accomplished seamstress. She was now the owner of a successful fashion salon. Separated from her husband for some time, she was waiting for her divorce.

In the middle of May, 1958, when Georg Puchert visited the German Federal Republic, the Seidenschnurs were already separated. She remained in Frankfurt; he moved to Bonn. There he was employed as representative for a group of Belgian arms manufacturers at their Bonn office.

The Seidenschnurs maintained only slight contact. Therefore, Els Seidenschnur did not immediately learn of Georg Puchert's visit to her husband.

The initial meeting between Puchert and Seidenschnur was brief. Captain Morris was much too careful to put his cards on the table immediately; he first explored the situation.

Although time was pressing and the situation in Wilaya 5 did not warrant delay, Puchert had to act unhurried.

"Contact man" Seidenschnur left a splendid impression with Puchert. He represented the Belgian armaments industry, and seemed to have excellent connections—even with speed-boat suppliers. His prices were favorable, and he had, apparently, no reservations about doing business with the Algerian rebels.

Still, Puchert waited four weeks before revealing his intended purchases: four or five high-powered speedboats, in first-class condition, with the option to buy more later; 1½ to 2 million rounds of infantry ammunition; 100 mortars with 10,000 rounds of ammunition; 2,000 automatic pistols with 3 million rounds; 2,000 9-mm pistols with 2 million rounds; 10,000 hand grenades; several thousand detonators with and without electric primers; several thousand yards of fuse cord; 20,000 rounds of phosphoric signal cartridges and, most important, a minimum of 200 tons of TNT (trinitrotoluene).

Seidenschnur's eyes popped. This promised to be a multimillion-dollar deal! On the infantry and pistol ammunition alone he could easily make $65,000. Puchert's price for TNT would yield a clear profit of $2,125 per ton. And the requested 200 tons would give him, after deducting all expenses, a profit of $300,000. Excited anticipation of fantastic prospects kept Seidenschnur awake. Day and night he counted his profits over and over—if nothing went wrong . . .

It was most important to keep Puchert happy and away from all possible competition. Puchert had been traveling too much lately, to Hamburg, Zurich, Vienna, Cologne, Frankfurt, and Munich, and Seidenschnur was, to say the least, concerned. But now Puchert was ready for a few days' rest; he would review the details, and then the order would finally be placed. On June 16, 1958, at the Rheinhotel Dreesen in Bad Godesberg, next door to the French Embassy, the speedboat purchases would be discussed fully.

Seidenschnur had an idea. He called his wife in Frankfurt.

Could she get away for a few days and join him at Rheinhotel Dreesen? Her own future, the education of their children, security for her old age—everything was at stake, he told her in urgent, even tearful voice. But Els Seidenschnur was not easy to convince. Would he please be more precise? she asked icily.

Seidenschnur complied: A really important customer had turned up, immensely wealthy, very serious, and a tremendous business deal could be concluded, a deal that would happen only once in a lifetime. Negotiations were in their final stage; only a few details had to be cleared up. But just these small details, if they turned out well, could mean an extra $150,000 or perhaps $200,000. But even if the worst should happen, he would still make a profit of $500,000 on the deal, an amount that should interest her, at least a little, regardless of her feelings for him.

What was her role in the deal? Els wanted to know. To wish him luck? That she could do in Frankfurt.

Now Seidenschnur applied his strongest persuasion. There should be some "atmosphere" during these last decisive negotiations. A little female charm could work miracles. She should think of the children, her own future. Would she want to be sorry later?

Els had no desire to regret a lost opportunity, so she asked for some advance travel money. And she would not have been a woman had she not added, "I have nothing to wear!"

Seidenschnur, the prospective millionaire, was in a generous mood: "I will telegraph $200. You are so understanding —and you will not regret it. Take the express train, tomorrow at noon!"

The next day, Els Seidenschnur, wearing a stunning creation from her own fashion salon, matching shoes, and a new hairstyle, boarded the train to Bad Godesberg.

She did not expect much, perhaps a few relaxing days in an international hotel away from her everyday routine and worries. She was also a bit curious to meet the man who wanted to buy millions of dollars' worth of weapons. Later, she would have no regrets.

It was her husband who would regret the arrangement.

So far, everything went according to Seidenschnur's plan.

Puchert was somewhat reserved; gradually he became more relaxed, and the tension from constant danger eased. Seidenschnur had never before seen him so charming. No doubt Captain Morris found his associate's wife attractive. And this was exactly Seidenschnur's plan. It was decided to postpone business for the day and to enjoy a gay and relaxed evening. Dinner was excellent, as were the wines and, later, the champagne. Els had ample opportunity to learn of Puchert's ability on the dance floor, and he in turn found his partner exceedingly charming. As the evening progressed, he was not at all shocked to learn that she stayed at the hotel, and not with her husband, from whom she had been separated, expecting to be granted a divorce in the near future.

Seidenschnur had left.

Late the next day they returned to business. Some of the merchandise (the speedboats) was to be ordered later. Still, Seidenschnur was more than satisfied. He was to supply 1½ million rounds of infantry ammunition and 40 tons of TNT.

Els was also present, looking absolutely charming. Again and again Puchert's eyes wandered to her admiringly.

Seidenschnur thought that Els was a very attractive woman and that today she looked ten years younger. He completely forgot his pending divorce. He folded the contract and put it in his elegant morocco case. He was satisfied with himself and the world in general. Georg Puchert pressed Els Seidenschnur's hand gently. Seidenschnur congratulated himself; his speculations had worked out beautifully.

But this conclusion was drawn too hastily. Things turned out to be slightly different. The tough man from Tangier fell in love with Els. That could have been expected. He placed fat orders with Seidenschnur. That also could have been expected. But Els developed a genuine affection for Puchert. That, definitely, was not expected. Seidenschnur's pride and self-assurance were terribly hurt, but he decided to ignore the situation.

Until the day he found an empty envelope unmistakably in Puchert's handwriting. To anyone else it would have been meaningless. Still, the discovery destroyed Seidenschnur's composure completely, and, in all its consequences, would have catastrophic effects on European weapons traffic, for the sender's address on the envelope was Georg Puchert, c/o Seidenschnur, Lindenstrasse 3, Frankfurt am Main.

Seidenschnur did not show his rage openly. During the summer months he and Puchert became nearly inseparable business partners.

Many transactions, large and small—discussed later in this book—were to be negotiated and completed. During an incredibly short time Seidenschnur supplied nearly the entire needs of Puchert's North African friends. There were pistols, hand grenades, machine guns, and mines.

Other merchandise took longer to obtain, especially the urgently needed TNT—ordinary explosives were readily available, but TNT was a military explosive, and much more difficult to get.

But Seidenschnur persisted because profits were attractive. He was searching for new connections, with Scandinavia, for example, where there were TNT manufacturers prepared to accept orders for their merchandise. It was then that Seidenschnur met Ragnar Lie, a Norwegian with close connections with explosives factories in Norway.

Els Seidenschnur and Georg Puchert became nearly inseparable. Captain Morris lived permanently at Lindenstrasse 3; he even had his office there. He devoted considerable time to the education of the Seidenschnur children, looked after Els's income tax, the children's report cards, and even repaired the apartment's electrical installations. Sometimes, Els accompanied him on trips.

By the end of July, negotiations between Seidenschnur and Lie had reached the delivery stage. Seidenschnur had already contacted shipping and insurance companies.

He received quotations for shipping 40 tons of mining explosives and 85 tons of sporting ammunition for dispatch from Norway to Liberia—for the blasting of shipwrecks in the port of Monrovia, so he said, and for the many big-game hunters coming to Africa.

The shipping company and the freight and insurance brokers readily accepted the unlikely explanation. Although 40 tons of explosives would be sufficient to level the whole town of Monrovia, and 85 tons of sporting ammunition would be enough to exterminate all the elephants, rhinos, and buffalo of the entire African continent, they showed no concern; neither did the banks responsible for the monetary transaction, so long as it appeared "legal." And there was, of course, the profit angle to consider. . . .

Bartering for premiums and percentages and checking the numerous shipping and other documents took until the end of September.

And then the whole carefully built-up organization around the multimillion-dollar transaction blew up—as far as Seidenschnur's part in it was concerned. Georg Puchert contacted Lie and his Norwegian explosives supplier directly, and dropped Seidenschnur.

This vengeful measure was the result of an anonymous letter received toward the end of September by several foreign government agencies. In part it read:

Georg Puchert, called Morris, residing in Tangier, Morocco, 7 Rue Vermeer, married, one child, residing in Germany since the end of July, 1958, is a buyer of arms and ammunition for the FLN.

The report continued over several single-spaced typewritten pages and described Puchert's past, from smuggling cigarettes in the Mediterranean to the recent weapons transactions in Germany. The names and descriptions of several contact men of German and Algerian nationality were openly mentioned. It also contained a detailed description of the autos driven by Puchert and his business partners.

One contact man was conspicuously missing, his first and most important: Hans Joachim Seidenschnur.

He was not mentioned at all, and consequently all Puchert's activities for those three months with Seidenschnur, and his arrival in Germany in May, 1958, were completely missing in the report. The author had simply altered the facts.

Those receiving the document included the Frankfurt Police Headquarters, the Federal Bureau of Investigation in Bonn, the Moroccan Embassy in Bad Godesberg, and a French organization whose main task was to prevent illegal weapons traffic to Algeria.

Puchert, hearing about the letter through Moroccan friends, was dismayed.

The German police authorities added the document to their files, but took no action.

And Els Seidenschnur filed officially for divorce.

The weapons transactions on behalf of Wilaya 5, after some slight procedural changes, continued.

But the reaction of the French was quite different. They prepared to destroy Captain Morris's organization and to paralyze the arms traffic to Algeria's rebel areas.

On October 1, 1958, in the port of Hamburg, the German freighter *Atlas* was grounded by an explosives charge. And at about the same time, on an Ostend wharf, a magnetic charge exploded on the hull of the Egyptian freighter *Alkahira*. Both ships carried Puchert's cargo—destination North Africa.

The first major blow, however, fell on November 5, 1958, in Bad Godesberg. It struck a man unconnected with weapons transactions. On the Bonn-Godesberg expressway, called the "racetrack of the Diplomatic Corps," an attack unique in Germany's criminal history took place. On that morning, two cars closed in on a third, flanking it, forcing the driver to reduce speed. At the entrance to the Tunisian Embassy, the marked man's destination, an automatic gun began to hammer. The driver of the middle car slumped across the wheel, critically wounded, the car crashing into the Embassy door. Before anyone in the area could be alerted, the attackers had disappeared.

Only the wounded man remained. He was identified as Amédiane Ait Ahcène, twenty-seven years of age, a lawyer, member of the General Staff of the Algerian Revolutionary Committee, head of the unofficial FLN agency in Bonn. After a long hospitalization in Tunis, he died.

It was obvious that those responsible for the brutal attack had political motives. The German Federal Republic, Tunisia, and Algeria's FLN would all be embarrassed, negotiations would be disturbed, and German sympathizers of the FLN would be alarmed.

The gunshots were directed also against the weapons traffic, despite the fact that the young FLN diplomat was in no way connected with it. It was a demonstration of the reckless power and brutality of the weapons dealers' opponents. The slaying on the expressway was a last warning: They would shrink at nothing, even in the light of day and in city traffic. They did not respect diplomatic integrity, and they did not fear the police.

Coinciding with the attack, some of Puchert's most intimate business associates received letters, calls, and visitors. Purpose and method were always the same. The dealers were advised to retire from the weapons traffic, at least for the duration of the Algerian war. Compensation for the loss of profit would be generous.

The campaign to cut off Algeria's weapons supplies was brilliantly organized and had great psychological impact. First a powerful shock, a substantial threat, then a golden path to carefree living—the offer of big money without effort or risk.

Surprisingly, not all accepted. But this miracle can easily be explained: Georg Puchert knew his partners well. He told them not to believe in promises accompanied by a gun in hand; he intimidated them when they considered betrayal; and he then played his highest trump, always most effective in weapons traffic—higher prices.

In broad daylight:
Algeria's shadow ambassador Ait Ahcène fell victim
to the Red Hand on the Bonn–Godesberg expressway.

Photo: Petra Engelmann, Hamburg

Puchert's French adversaries indirectly accomplished their task. Puchert had to pay more; consequently he could buy less because the financial resources of the FLN were not unlimited.

In addition, Puchert knew that he was known and, of course, watched. His movements became more restricted.

The anonymous letter—Puchert had no doubt as to the identity of the author—provided his invisible enemies with numerous hints about Captain Morris's contacts, plans, and habits.

He had to be much more careful. Though the net around him was wide and loose, it could be tightened at any moment.

On the first Saturday in December, Puchert was in Frankfurt, planning some Christmas shopping with Els. It was four weeks since the attack on Ait Ahcène; the Bonn police were still searching for the gunman and his accomplices. His description was known: average height, heavy build, a boxer face with dark complexion and a knife scar extending from his right cheekbone to his mouth. Also known was his nickname, "Pedro." Pedro was thought to have disappeared across the border.

Puchert was not so sure about that. His instinct warned him of threatening danger. He was not even surprised when two figures blocked his way in the almost dark street, interposing between him and Els.

No Christmas shopping today, he thought, and reached for the gun in the holster under his left shoulder. But his winter coat was in the way. Before he could get to his Beretta, he felt the cold muzzle of a Colt in his neck.

"Don't move and nothing will happen," one of them said in Puchert's ear.

Accustomed to delicate situations, Captain Morris realized the futility of resistance.

"Go ahead slowly," he said quietly to Els, who was not aware of his situation. "I have to discuss some business for a few moments."

Els Seidenschnur, suspecting nothing, walked on.

The second man was of average height, heavy built. A scar across his cheek was evident.

"My name is Pedro," he said, introducing himself with an ironical little bow. "I am sure you've heard of me."

Puchert nodded. He now was convinced that there was no immediate danger. If he were to be executed, it would be over by now, without formalities. Apparently they both wanted only a friendly chat with him, despite the Colt pressed against his neck.

Pedro presented the demand: that Puchert get out of the weapons traffic. He need not betray anyone and he need make no financial sacrifice. His secrets were known. If he consented, he would be generously compensated for all loss.

"Does this include my recent losses also?" asked Puchert, stalling for time.

"But of course," replied Pedro, "you will also be paid for your cutters the *Bruja Roja* and the *Sirocco*."

"All right," said Puchert quickly, "I'll think it over. Call me next week and we'll arrange for another meeting."

He stepped aside quickly to get away from the cold muzzle against his neck. The man behind followed, but on Pedro's orders stepped back.

"I hope we understand each other perfectly, Monsieur," said Pedro. "This offer is also our last warning. If you continue this business, or think you can fool us, there will be some shooting here or, better, in Tangier. We hear you have a very pretty daughter there."

He smirked at Puchert and watched him intently. But Puchert kept his poker face.

Don't give yourself away, he thought, while fear for Marina's safety choked him.

"Stop this nonsense," he said curtly; "this is a deal."

"We hope so," answered Pedro politely. "See you Monday."

"What, so soon?" Puchert had expected to have at least about ten days.

"We're in a hurry," warned Pedro, and disappeared with his henchman.

Puchert's glance followed them while he rubbed his neck, where only a short while ago the cold muzzle of the Colt had touched his skin.

"Were those people business acquaintances?" asked Els.

"They would like to be," he said, smilingly.

The next morning, Sunday, December 7, 1958, Puchert traveled to Bonn. He had an appointment at the Hotel Königshof with Ragnar Lie. TNT was desperately needed, and Lie had connections with the manufacturer. Lie arrived after a long delay. He seemed extremely nervous. Hastily he drank a double Steinhäger, then another.

Puchert watched him carefully. This Norwegian drinks far too much, he thought.

"They are after me," Lie whispered. "They threatened to kill me. . . ."

Bit by bit, Puchert extracted the whole story. The French had approached Lie, made a similar offer, and issued the same warning Puchert received. The next weekend, Lie was expected to meet with them in Paris at the Hotel George V. The kind and amount of his compensation would be discussed there. But Lie was afraid. In the presence of Puchert, Lie called his French contact, Jean-Paul Mesmer, who was in Paris. Puchert remembered the number.

"I would rather meet you in Zurich, where I shall be next Thursday, in any event. Let's say 3:00 P.M. in the lobby of the Schwiezerhof?" Mesmer agreed.

Puchert realized that he had lost a business partner. But he asked, "Are we still in the TNT business?"

Lie hesitated. After all, the first shipment was ready for dispatch in Drammen. The profit to him would be about $65,-000. Lie thought of the money, and then remembered the people who pointed a knife at his throat but who offered him the same amount in compensation, $65,000. If he wanted only the $65,-000, there would be no hesitation.

But Lie wanted more: the profit *and* the compensation.

He had another double Steinhäger, and decided: "We'll complete this one transaction—and then I quit!"

Puchert nodded agreeably. He had his own ideas.

They then discussed the details.

The next morning Puchert was extremely busy. He had to announce the TNT shipment in Morocco, obtain the letter of credit, and approve the insurance policies. But still he found time to call Monsieur Mesmer in Paris. Not as Georg Puchert or Captain Morris, of course, but "calling for Director Lie."

"The director is terribly sorry to postpone the meeting scheduled for Thursday. He will be in Zurich Saturday, at the same time, the same place."

Mesmer agreed. Puchert was very satisfied as he put the receiver back.

Puchert made another important call that day—to Els Seidenschnur in Frankfurt. He was happy to hear that all was well, no mail, no visitors, no important calls—only one gentleman called: named Pedro, who said he would call back.

On Tuesday morning Puchert called Frankfurt again. This time Els was very alarmed. "I'm glad you called," she said. "This Pedro makes me nervous. Yesterday he phoned three times, and once again this morning. He talks as if he were ridiculing you, and then makes all sorts of hidden threats. Will you be back soon?"

"As soon as possible," promised Puchert. "Some time today. But don't tell Pedro about it. Give him my regards, and tell him that I had to go on a trip to another country but that our agreement still stands. This is important: It still stands!"

But when Puchert arrived in Frankfurt, he was met at the railway gates. Two men, smiling cheerfully, took hold of his arms in an iron grip, and greeted him like old friends—Pedro on his left, the other on his right.

"Back already?" inquired Pedro, grinning.

The situation required quick thinking. Only an enormous bluff could help Puchert.

"Let me go, you idiots!" he warned. "Do you want to create a scene here? The railway station is teeming with *fellaghas!* If the *Ratons* see us together, our beautiful plan goes up in smoke —then the République Française can save millions, and has only to pay for our funeral."

With this speech, this rude abuse of his friends, Puchert had a dual purpose: The two gunmen must believe that he had changed sides and that he was already even thinking and talking like them. And he wanted them—without threatening—to think that they would not have a chance should there be a shooting at the railway station. His plan succeeded. The two looked around, spotted a few Algerians, and released him.

The Algerians were harmless refugees from France, working as laborers in Germany. They always spent part of their spare time at the railway station because there they could meet compatriots to discuss news from home, and they could buy French newspapers. They were complete strangers to Puchert, but of course Pedro and his accomplice were unaware of it.

Puchert used his advantage.

"I'll see you in ten minutes, over there in the movie theater, first row," he whispered to Pedro, and disappeared in the crowd.

Now they'll think I've disappeared, Puchert reasoned, and when I turn up in the theater, they'll trust me.

Fifteen minutes later, Puchert and Pedro sat side by side, facing the screen under the flickering light of a gangster movie. The walls reverberated from the nonstop shooting. Puchert whispered his master plan in Pedro's ear, a plan he had contrived during the last ten minutes: He, Puchert, did not like the way things were going. The style was amateurish. He was prepared to quit, but it had to be worth his while. He would not be satisfied with a few thousand dollars. He would be willing, however, to break up the entire Algerian organization, but he would require $250,000 to do so, and an equal amount as compensation for lost profits.

But that was not all: "At the end of January, at the latest by the middle of February, I'll have at my disposal more than

$1,250,000—*fellagha* money, which I'll take with me to Australia, when I quit here. Then I'll have close to $2,000,000. That should be enough."

Pedro began to object, but he was curious, just as Puchert had figured. Puchert continued: "Without this money, the *fellaghas* will be high and dry. You get what you want, and so do I, without any trouble. And you, son," he said slowly, watching Pedro from the corners of his eyes, "you'll receive a reward for your patience. To you I'll leave the reserve I brought from Tangier, for emergencies." He paused for a moment. Pedro's eyes were glued to Puchert's lips. He had swallowed the bait. "It's $200,000 in cash, a great deal of money, and you have to wait only a few months for it."

Pedro thought it over. It would be difficult to put off his employer for ten, perhaps twelve, weeks. On the other hand, $200,000 was a lot of money. He could buy a sweet little nightclub in Brussels.

"OK," he said finally, "but hurry up—and no tricks. I'll be around wherever you go. And don't forget, there's Miss Marina in Tangier."

With this threat, he left. Puchert remained, and breathed freely again.

The gangsters on the screen, surrounded by police, retreated to a vacant manufacturing plant. "We've got to stall for time," the gangster boss screamed, "if we're going to make it!"

Puchert smiled. That was exactly his plan. He had no intention of betrayal. He would put off the enemy for two or three months, and then retreat. If we're going to make it, he thought.

For some time everything went smoothly. Two sizable shipments of arms arrived safely in North Africa. But then trouble began. Lie pulled out, and Puchert's well-defined plan went astray. His trick to prevent Lie's meeting with Mesmer did not work. On Thursday, in Zurich, Lie waited in vain for the French agent. Consuming quantities of Steinhäger, and becoming increasingly nervous, he waited another day. But the man from Paris never arrived.

Is it too late to pull out? Lie asked himself with mounting despair.

When he finally arrived home, his fear had grown so great that at his next encounter with the French agent he offered no resistance.

Puchert's second setback stemmed from the first: A few days before Christmas, the Danish freighter *Granita,* on the way to Casablanca, was stopped by French destroyers, searched, and ordered to the port of Mersel-Kébir. There the cargo was confiscated: 40 tons of TNT—Lie's first part-shipment for Wilaya 5.

The Christmas and New Year holidays were peaceful at Lindenstrasse 3 in Frankfurt.

Although Els had a sense of impending danger, she could not define it. Pedro did not call again.

About the middle of January, she accompanied Puchert on a trip to Bonn. Late at night they visited a small, intimate bar, the Hedgehog at Fuerstenstrasse, which was popular with the younger set of Bonn's diplomatic circles. Puchert hoped to meet the commercial attaché of a South American country, from whom he wanted a favor.

Instead, he met other acquaintances. A disreputable-looking French-speaking group crowded around a table. The loud one among them was a man with the scarred face of a boxer, Pedro.

Conversation stopped as Puchert and Els entered. Pedro gave Puchert a quizzical look.

Is it wise to appear at this place? he seemed to ask.

Puchert nodded—in greeting or agreement—and left.

He and Els drove off in a sand-colored Mercedes 190, which Puchert had recently purchased.

"Who are those people?" asked Els.

"The man with the scar is Pedro," said Puchert softly, while they drove through the quiet streets of West Germany's capital. "He's a dangerous man, but I hope I've tamed him. The tall, dark man beside him, who looks like Elvis Presley with padded shoulders, is Jean Viari, ex-police inspector of the special brigade at Casablanca, nicknamed *le tueur,* the killer."

Els was alarmed. "For God's sake, what kind of people are they?"

"The others I don't know," Puchert replied dryly, "neither the little Napoléon Buonaparte character nor the gray-haired man. But no doubt they're Pedro's friends, and I'm on their blacklist."

That night, Puchert told Els the whole story—everything he knew about Pedro and his associates. He mentioned only briefly his weapons-buying mission, and he touched fleetingly on the betrayal by Lie.

He dwelt longer on his concern for Marina.

"Ask her to come and stay with us here," said Els.

The next morning Puchert wired to Tangier, and a few days later Marina, a seventeen-year-old, self-confident young lady, arrived at Lindenstrasse 3 on her first trip to Europe.

For a few days, all danger was forgotten while father and daughter celebrated their reunion. Marina adjusted quickly to the situation. She made friends with Els, and they went out together to shops and to dances.

February passed quickly.

On the morning of February 27, Puchert had another meeting with the impatient Pedro. They met in a small café in the heart of Frankfurt. The conversation was heated, but in the end, Puchert thought he had put Pedro off again.

Looking in a mirror, he noticed a man who seemed to have been following their conversation very attentively. He was dressed conservatively, wearing a black Homburg and carrying a folded umbrella; he was not very tall, but of athletic build, with wide cheekbones and intelligent eyes. Puchert was terrified when he saw the man signaling to Pedro—a slight nod—his death warrant.

By the time Puchert left, the man had gone. But he knew

the significance of his appearance—it was his feared opponent, the French Intelligence colonel Marcel Mercier, whose mission was the destruction of the Algerian supply lines. He sometimes called himself Jean-Paul Mesmer.

Puchert now realized that his game with Pedro was over, his time was up. That evening, he sent the following note to his closest associate, the Algerian Abdelkader Noassri:

Am very concerned, am being followed; had a bad surprise (Mercier!). Must see you urgently. Morris.

During the next days, Puchert's activities were hectic. He knew that every hour was precious. Within a week, everything must be wound up or passed on to Noassri. Then he could leave with Marina, first for Vienna, then to the Balkans. In two or three months, a new start would be possible. To top it all, he felt the first signs of influenza.

On the evening of March 2, on the way home from a long drive, he felt ill. He had a temperature, and his head and joints ached. Because of the heavy traffic, his progress was painfully slow. Spotting a parking space in Guiolettstrasse—five minutes from the Lindenstrasse apartment—he decided to leave his car there. Usually it was parked in a pay garage, in a locked single compartment. Just once won't cost me my head, thought Puchert. Like thousands of cars parked on Frankfurt's streets, particularly now during the Trade Fair, he left his Mercedes, for this one night, exposed.

While Puchert was in bed, taking aspirins for his cold, his enemies were taking advantage of the opportunity. The next morning, at nine, Puchert left the house, his legs still a bit shaky, but his head was clear. On the way to his car he bought a paper and cigarettes. At 9:11 he unlocked his car and slipped behind the wheel.

It took forty seconds for the cold engine to begin to purr. He let it idle for a while, and then put it into first gear.

At exactly 9:12 he drove off.

He had moved only a few feet when a heavy explosion shook the street. Windows shattered. Schoolchildren walking by were thrown to the ground; splinters and car parts whirled through the air. The pedestrians on the busy street did not know which way to turn. No one was injured, apart from Georg Puchert, who was now slumped over the wheel, bleeding to death from thousands of steel pellets and fragments, his body pressed against the horn of the torn car, causing a horrible, shrill, continuous sound.

For minutes there was only the piercing sound of the horn. Then a pedestrian picked up enough courage to lift the dead Captain Morris from the wheel. The horn fell silent, while police cars raced to the scene of the assassination, their sirens screaming.

THE BONN
LIAISON OFFICE

POLICE ENGAGED IN SOLVING A MAJOR crime are seldom favorably inclined toward inquisitive people; they themselves are inquisitive. And if they are working on an assassination case involving political motives, they reject all intrusions.

Every reporter knows this, and therefore I was not very hopeful when I visited the Frankfurt Homicide Squad. But to my astonishment the officers of the First Squad showed understanding and patience. Considering the late hour of my visit and the fact that I did not know any of them, I was somewhat pleasantly surprised by the friendly reception.

However, their cooperation might have been partly the result of a recent unsolved crime, the violent murder of a widely known and, after her death, world-famous young woman with the unusual name of Rosemary Nitribitt. This unsolved murder, which did not help to promote police popularity, might have softened their normally brusque attitude, or perhaps they were still so much in the dark in the Puchert case that they welcomed anyone who could provide even seemingly insignificant clues or hints; then, again, perhaps they were simply just pleasant, cooperative police officers.

After working hours we all had a couple of beers together, talked on a variety of subjects, came to the subject of mutual interest, and finally agreed to a nonobligatory exchange of ideas on some aspects of the assassination. No, this was not to be a collaboration between the police and a reporter such as one sees in the movies or reads in a novel.

Police investigations are confidential, and officers cannot, on their own, release any information to a reporter; however, a journalist's duty is to provide the public with fast and reliable information, not to play detective. Nevertheless, police and reporters sometimes pull on the same rope, harass each other a little, or even exchange some interesting information, especially if one party is sure that the other will not take advantage of the knowledge acquired that way.

I was favorably impressed by the First Squad, and in addition I obtained some useful information, for instance, the address of the head of the household at Lindenstrasse 3—Hans Joachim Seidenschnur.

The next morning I traveled to Bonn, and that day met Seidenschnur in the lobby of the Königshof, the preferred meeting place of Bonn's businessmen, diplomats, and politicians. Seidenschnur—tall, broad-shouldered, impeccably groomed, in his late forties—appeared gentlemanly and jovial. He seemed to be the dynamic manager type with great appreciation for the *joie de vivre,* the businessman with international connections and experience, the big boss whose reckless demeanor was hidden by an expensive, custom-tailored suit.

His business card read:

Hans Joachim Seidenschnur
Managing Director and Legal Adviser
Syndicate of Belgian Armaments Manufacturers
Bonn Liaison Office

"Did you know Georg Puchert?" I began the conversation. Seidenschnur smiled. He opened his dark green morocco

Hans Joachim Seidenschnur:
an elegant personality in the international weapons market; prefers slender women and large business deals.

Photo: Max Ehlert, Hamburg

leather briefcase, bearing the gold initials HJS, and handed me a copy of an anonymous letter, received in October, 1958, by several German and other national governments, informing them in detail of Puchert's history and activities.

I was speechless.

"I wrote that letter," explained the legal adviser, smiling. He sipped his Martini and added coolly, without my having asked for his motives, "People like Puchert and their dirty business have to be destroyed!"

"With auto bombs?" I asked politely.

"Of course not! I detest such direct methods! But if the authorities had intervened sooner, if they had not discarded my warnings as unimportant, all this excitement would have been avoided."

It was not the sudden death of Captain Morris that Seidenschnur regretted, but the possible involvement of himself and others caused by the violent end of his former business associate.

"Did it have to go that far?" the armaments manufacturers' representative continued pathetically, fishing an olive from his cocktail glass, and looking at me expectantly.

I did not reply. After he had eaten the little fruit and dried his manicured fingers on a handkerchief matching his silk tie, he continued: "Was this necessary? Should the Algerians be permitted to settle their grievances with explosives on the open roads of Germany?"

"Do you think the Algerian FLN killed their own chief buyer?"

"Yes, of course!" replied Seidenschnur hastily. "It is probable that Puchert wanted to quit or that the Algerians discovered that he spent their war funds for his own purposes."

"You are, of course, a little prejudiced against Captain Morris," I said, interrupting Seidenschnur's speculations, "but I'm surprised that you should have these same feelings against the Algerians. After all, the FLN is one of your customers."

I had expected to see Seidenschnur fly into a rage. But he did not seem offended; he laughed happily.

"Oh, yes, I had some minor transactions with them. We in

the weapons business cannot be choosy and we cannot ask too many questions. But my transactions were and are always strictly legal. Therefore, I don't consider the Algerian rebels to be my customers."

"We'd better forget about that," I suggested. "My interest, at present, is concentrated on a different matter. I'm trying to find out whether there is any connection between Puchert's assassination and previous similar bombings. I also want to know more about Puchert's business deals, his methods, his suppliers, his reputation among his associates and in his field in general. And, finally, I want to find out whether it is worthwhile to be a weapons dealer, considering the risks."

Seidenschnur did not hesitate long. If his own part in the business was not mentioned, he was quite willing to share his extensive knowledge with me.

"I have no information about possible connections between the Puchert bombing and previous cases," he began. "I have given it no thought and am not particularly interested in that aspect. But I am quite familiar with Puchert's business practices. And this answers your last question as to whether such business is worthwhile. I can tell you stories to make your eyes pop!"

"I shall be very obliged," I replied courteously, but such encouragement was not necessary. Seidenschnur was in his element, and nothing could stop him.

He named Puchert's suppliers, explained every transaction, with the exact quantities, prices, and other data. And when his excellent memory failed, he consulted his notebook.

Later, when we continued our conversation at the elegantly furnished liaison office, Seidenschnur supported his revelations with copies of business correspondence. He showed me stacks of files with samples of correspondence I could not have imagined in my wildest dreams.

There, honest Swiss liqueur manufacturers and hotel proprietors offered between "Dear Sir" and "Very sincerely yours" large quantities of "arsenal-fresh Teller mines" and "brand-new, carefully preserved tiger tanks."

Honorable members of the legal fraternity in West Germany's major cities offered "machine guns in first-class NATO condition FOB Trieste or Hamburg," or advertised their services "to supply every desired quantity of infantry ammunition in all available East or West calibers."

Members, including ladies, of the German high aristocracy politely referred "to your esteemed request for mortars," or offered, at favorable terms, "a large quantity of hand grenades and 10,000 automatic pistols, model Schmeisser."

And officials of Iron Curtain state-owned organizations made every effort to win customers among the Western capitalists, offering weapons and ammunition of every brand and type, against hard currency, of course, despite the fact that these prospective customers were imperialist warmongers and plutocrats.

"Did Puchert buy from all these sources?" I asked Seidenschnur doubtfully. It seemed Captain Morris could have armed to the teeth the whole nonwhite world with only a tenth of this enormous stock, and could have obtained the supplies for Wilaya 5 without any difficulties.

"Well," my informative partner said smilingly, "some of these offers should not be taken too seriously. Some are business offers by people who don't keep any stock, just middlemen. When they receive an order, they look around for a supplier. But such methods are most despicable."

Seidenschnur wrinkled his bushy brows and extended his strong lower lip contemptuously. "But," he continued, "these practices are not too unusual. Most of them"—he rapped on the top file cover of this strange business correspondence—"are absolutely serious, for example, this one." He handed me a letter by the Czech government-owned export agency "Omnipol." "This was a deal! A pretty thing! I regret that Puchert did not use my services there!"

The "pretty thing" where to his regret Seidenschnur had been left out had taken place in Jungholz, a small, popular resort town in southern Bavaria, to be exact, in the Tyrol. Where customs and economics are concerned, Jungholz is under the jurisdiction of the West German Government, but the territory itself is part of the Republic of Austria.

This circumstance was favorable for Puchert's transaction. Guns and automatic weapons from Czechoslovakia were smuggled through the woods in minibuses to the quiet, idyllic town, carefully avoiding the customs and border controls. In Jungholz, where Captain Morris was vacationing, he received the Czech merchandise: 40 small crates with 50.08 caliber pistols in each; 100 packages with 10 model Schmeisser automatic pistols in each. The Schmeisser is a proved weapon manufactured for export in government-owned Czech Communist factories, and stamped with a well-known German trademark.* Georg Puchert paid cash for this shipment, piece by piece—$12 for each pistol and $18 for each automatic pistol.

Incidentally, the weapons were sold to representatives of the Algerian underground organization in France—not to his regular employer, Wilaya 5—who prepared themselves for a wave of terror attacks, requiring, besides explosives, mainly small arms.

Captain Morris's relationship with the French Algerians was devoid of any cordial feelings; he did not hesitate to adjust his prices accordingly, considering also the fact that the so-called *"Fédération de France,"* the principal organization of the Algerian underground in France, had unlimited funds at its disposal. Every one of the 400,000 Algerian workers in France was forced to contribute 10 percent of his weekly earnings to these funds.

After receiving the merchandise in Jungholz, Puchert dispatched it by rail to the Saarland–French border, still within German territory, without the risk of control.

From there it was the responsibility of the *Fédération de*

---

* The 98K Mauser rifle, used by the German Army in World War II, is still in great demand by revolutionaries all over the world. A high-priced weapon in the trade, it is still being manufactured in Czechoslovakia. The brand-new weapons are stamped with the insignia of the Third Reich, including the swastika, old firing marks, and a Second World War date. They are sold as "genuine."

France—whose members knew the secret channels across the French border. But before this last stage, a representative of the French underground organization would deliver a suitcase full of money to the "vacationing" Puchert: $40 for each pistol, $65 for each automatic pistol.

This comparatively small-scale transaction, without any particular risk or effort for Puchert, netted a profit of exactly $173,500.

No wonder Seidenschnur's sorrows were genuine!

No wonder also that he was jealous of Puchert's easy spoils, but he did not know then—and neither did I—that Captain Morris's profit margin on all transactions on behalf of Wilaya 5, whose situation was desperate, was only a small fraction of what he dared to ask from the wealthy Algerian underground organization in France.

My first, very revealing conversation with Seidenschnur lasted the whole day, and toward evening I invited him to dinner. Being frivolous, I left the task of choosing the menu to him. While I made some phone calls, he studied the wine list, then the menu, and conducted a lengthy, whispered conversation with the head-waiter, who went into a series of deep bows and very respectful glances. I had returned to the table without paying too much attention to these prolonged negotiations. Finally, with a radiant smile, he turned to me and asked, "Guess what we are having for dinner?" He rubbed his hands happily, and continued, "I won't say. It is going to be a surprise!"

It was. My employer's Accounting Department reimbursed me for this dinner only after a great deal of argument and persuasion on my part. The documentary evidence of the evening, provided with a gilded frame, became the most prominent wall decoration in the Accounting Department.

The meal began with a dozen oysters of the best quality and a bottle of Chablis, and proceeded with two modest cups of turtle broth, reaching its first climax with *truite bleu*. This was followed by *Tournedo Rossini,* half a turkey, sweetly interrupted by an appetizing salad of fresh asparagus and artichokes, small pies with a Russian caviar filling, truffles prepared each in a unique way, and also a platter with cheese, fresh fruit, mocha, and tiny pieces of pastry; then a specialty of the house, namely, iced crême flambéed with Scotch whisky and served with a bottle of Moët et Chandon of the best vintage, selected by Seidenschnur, who had also chosen the other excellent but expensive beverages befitting each gourmet course.

I had long given up, while he still continued enjoying the cuisine, trying to console me and my allegedly weak stomach with funny little tales of the German weapons merchant's life.

"I once had caviar pies like these with Georg Puchert in Switzerland," he said. "I think it was in Zurich. There we celebrated the successful conclusion of a business transaction for three nights and days—infantry ammunition for Casablanca, 8 million rounds. As Liaison Officer for the Syndicate of the Belgian Armaments Industry, I took the liberty of inviting our good customer Puchert to a gala dinner. And Puchert then invited me, his good supplier, to a little sip of champagne. Then it was my turn again, and fortunately the lady members of an Oriental dance group were staying in the same hotel."

Then followed an off-colored story about the two successful weapons merchants getting better acquainted with four of the most beautiful belly dancers. Seidenschnur's unfailing memory permitted me to become familiar with even the most intimate details of the events that had then taken place in Switzerland.

Our conversation would never have returned to the weapons traffic had the waiters not served the turkey, which immediately produced another chapter from Seidenschnur's memory: "Delicious," he commented, after putting a sizable piece on his plate, "absolutely excellent! But the turkey I had once in Hamburg—by the way, Puchert was there with me—tasted still better! At the time, Puchert had just dispatched a shipment of 40 tons of trinitrotoluene—declared as mining explosives, of course—on board the *Granita*. Yes, that was a turkey!"

Again he was overcome by his memories. With each course he opened up new aspects of the busy, restless life of the world's weapons dealers. I slowly gained the impression that the enormous risks involved, as well as the weapons merchants' fantastically high living, would certainly considerably influence their price margin.

How many uprisings and revolutions don't take place, I thought, because the weapons merchants' insatiable appetites make their wares simply too expensive!

But at the conclusion of our dinner, I had to revise these ideas: Not all the weapons merchants whose life stories Seidenschnur so generously reported (some of whom I met personally later, and my reports of these meetings will appear in this book) lived in such extravagance. Many led an average middle-class life, without princely dinner and expensive girl friends. And the high life of the extravagant type was not always the result of big and successful business deals; more often it was the opposite: These men were looking for fast and easy profits in the weapons traffic because they desired an extravagant life, and to fulfill this ambition they would risk almost anything.

There could be no doubt as to which category my gourmet guest belonged. He came from a respectable middle-class family. His father had advanced to Paymaster General in the Prussian Army. The son, born late in their life, received a good education. He graduated from the university and was to enter the civil service. Had he followed his parents' wish and become a high-ranking civil servant, his income would have been just enough to pay for his tailor, not to speak of gourmet dinners, luxury apartments, and champagne orgies with Oriental dancers.

But Hans Joachim Seidenschnur's ambition was to exploit the talents with which he had been endowed—his intelligence and organizational abilities—without monetary restrictions. So he landed in the weapons business—after some detours, of course. The legal basis was provided by the Bonn Agency for a syndicate of Belgian armaments manufacturers trying to obtain *Bundeswehr* (German Federal Army) contracts and which he had cleverly coordinated with his Liaison Office.

To obtain government contracts, however, without extremely close and powerful connections with high officials, is time-consuming and troublesome. Dr. Aloys Brandenstein, Seidenschnur's successor, the "Uncle Aloys" of West Germany's Defense Minister, Franz Josef Strauss, had important contacts, and would gain not only notoriety in West Germany but millions of dollars as well.

Although Seidenschnur was not yet a millionaire, he certainly lived like one. His extravagant ways had been financed partly by advances paid by the patiently waiting Belgian armaments manufacturers, and partly by the profits made through quick business deals with people of doubtful reputation who, on the edge of legality, wanted to dispose of certain quantities of merchandise from a seemingly inexhaustible reservoir of European weapons, and needed Seidenschnur's assistance.

But the prospective millionaire had waited in feverish expectation for the real "big deal." His only chance came in the spring of 1958 in the person of Captain Morris from Tangier. Just forty-eight hours ago this man had been assassinated by an auto bomb, and with him went Seidenschnur's bid to become a millionaire. Then how was it that the assassination, with all its consequences for Seidenschnur, left him comparatively cold, that he displayed no interest in who the suspected assassins might be? My talkative guest turned taciturn when I directed our conversation to the murder.

Again and again he would bring the conversation back to the manifold and profitable transactions conducted by the deceased. He openly described Puchert's plans, named his many assistants, middlemen, and suppliers, and told me joyfully all the tricks employed by Captain Morris and his friends to beat the law.

"These people should really be reported to the authorities," he said, and I was not sure whether his indignation was genuine or not. Apparently, the elegant liaison officer liked himself in the role of the serious business executive, despising the "dirty" competition.

"I'll help you to expose these smugglers and traffickers," I said.

But the first person he named led us again, in an elegant arc, back to an area where he did not want me to be: Puchert's murder as another link in a chain of identical cases.

Arriving at a subject Seidenschnur was so anxiously trying to avoid, namely, the instigators of the Frankfurt assassination, and other parallel cases, was achieved quite easily.

"Who was Puchert's first contact in Germany, not counting yourself? I asked.

He replied, without hesitation, "Otto Schlüter in Hamburg."

In Frankfurt a car had been bombed and a weapons dealer assassinated. One and a half years ago, in Hamburg, an attempt on the life of another weapons dealer had been made in exactly the same manner. His escape was more than narrow. And Seidenschnur, the weapons dealer, the gourmet who emphatically denied any connection between these two cases and similar ones, now provided the so far unknown, but strongest evidence for a connection between the two bombings. The intended Hamburg victim was an early business associate of the Frankfurt victim.

"Do you know Otto Schlüter?" I asked carefully.

"Yes, but not very well, " replied Seidenschnur, and ordered another Rémy-Martin with his mocha. "In our business circles he is called 'Otto the Strange One,' because of his rather extraordinary practices. But one thing is sure: He is a unique weapons expert. I can tell you quite a tale about 'Otto the Strange One.' "

Seidenschnur's stories about his colleague Otto Schlüter, and the astonishing particulars about him that I discovered in newspaper archives, were extraordinary, but my personal impression of him was even more amazing.

The morning following my dinner with Seidenschnur, I took the first flight to Hamburg, where until early afternoon I read all available articles and reports on Otto Schlüter—three overflowing files contained more information than I had ever hoped to find. I looked up his private and business addresses in the phone directory, and finally I paid Otto the Strange One an unannounced visit.

At that time, Schlüter had a large store in the "Cityhof," a group of multiple-story buildings near the main railway station. There he sold sporting guns and ammunition, binoculars, telescopes, blank cartridges, revolvers, and hunting knives —in short, all the merchandise one expects to find in a sporting-goods store, and, of course, small arms, if a police permit could be provided.

But my interests were limited to a personal meeting with the owner, and after I had stated this to a clerk, he led the way to a plainly furnished office at the rear of the store.

My reception was not particularly warm. Schlüter's experiences with inquisitive people had been distressing—as I was told later. Besides, he was in a hurry.

We then agreed to a meeting for the next day, which was conducted in a friendlier fashion, and during the next weeks and months we met quite frequently. What I had imagined about Schlüter and his life was corroborated more and more by the facts, and my first impression remained unchanged: Otto Schlüter, compared with his colleague Seidenschnur, was in most respects very different. Schlüter was an honest, modestly living businessman whose practices were not to dazzle but to impress people with a persistent thoroughness. He lived with his wife, children, and aged mother in a middle-class apartment, and dressed modestly, mostly in suits resembling a hunter's outfit, and wore sturdy shoes. And where the elegant Seidenschnur demanded caviar, lobster, and oysters, Otto Schlüter preferred a cabbage dish or, at the most, a venison stew.

Still, his life story is not only much more interesting than Seidenschnur's; it is also more revealing in respect to the weapons business.

OTTO
THE STRANGE ONE

OTTO SCHLÜTER WAS THE SCION of three generations of master gunsmiths. Grandfather Schlüter had been apprenticed to the Royal Prussian Arms Factory in Spandau, near Berlin. He worked there as a master gunsmith for many years until he left to establish his own business in the port of Rostock, which his son Otto II, also a master gunsmith, continued.

When Schlüter's grandson, Otto III, was born in 1920, the Schlüter gunsmith dynasty at Rostock had become fairly wealthy. After graduating from high school, Otto was apprenticed to the arms factories in Suhl and Zella-Mehlis, following the family tradition. But for World War II, Otto most likely would have continued the family line, enlarged its holdings, and lived out his life a prosperous respected citizen. Instead, he was destined to furnish glaring headlines for the international press.

In 1939, Otto was drafted, sent to the front, wounded twice in Russia, and in 1943 returned home, his right hand paralyzed. In 1944 he was ordered to lead a *Volkssturm* (Home Army) Company.

In the following year the Schlüter buildings in the center of town were bombed to rubble; their machinery and stocks were looted and dismantled by the Russians, and ultimately the manufacture and sale of weapons was prohibited. The Schlüters changed their occupation to the repair of bicycles and sewing machines.

Otto's father died after the war, and when Otto learned that the Russians were deporting arms specialists to Russia, he packed his belongings and fled with his wife, child, and mother to Schleswig-Holstein.

In 1947, he appeared in Ratzeburg, then Mölln, where he contributed to Germany's reconstruction by manufacturing shotguns, archery equipment, and handcuffs.

He had rented a large shed for this enterprise, situated on the site of a former ammunitions factory. Six years later, his Hubertus Metal Works went into bankruptcy. West Germany's demand for such merchandise was apparently insufficient to keep Schlüter in business long. But he was soon on his feet again. He obtained a Hamburg license to manufacture and sell arms and ammunition.

The new business was publicized for the first time on the evening of September 28, 1956, when a 5-kilogram bomb exploded on Schlüter's premises. Someone had mounted the bomb, disguised as a fire extinguisher and equipped with a time fuse, in his office rest room.

At the time of the explosion Schlüter was in an adjoining room, meeting with his business associates. His aged mother, who was present, was seriously injured in the blast. A sixty-two-year-old export agent, Wilhelm Lorenzen, was killed, while the others were only slightly injured. However, one person was unhurt: Otto Schlüter.

The assassins were never found, despite Schlüter's cooperation in the police investigation.

He consulted an occultist in the Netherlands, supposed to possess clairvoyant faculties, and followed up with a clergyman with a similar reputation in Würzburg. It was a considerable expense, but he hoped they could identify his attackers. But not even the fourth dimension provided any results. The

Otto Schlüter's premises:
above, after the bombing by the Red Hand;
below, Schlüter's new store.

Photos: Collection Bernt Engelmann

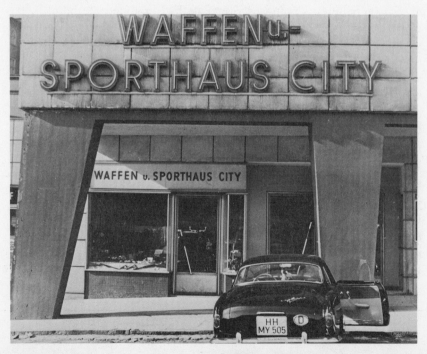

police investigation also proved fruitless, and public opinion turned against Schlüter.

Prodded by headlines of smear newspapers appealing to a half-literate audience, a general campaign against the weapons dealer seemed to materialize. His landlady was approached with the demand that she terminate his lease, and the license bureau was pressed to cancel his license.

A successful campaign, however, would need more evidence than that provided by the newspapers—Schlüter's past was investigated, the old bankruptcy was brought to light, and his stocks, books, and correspondence were audited repeatedly. Not the slightest discrepancy could be found to recommend prosecution.

Along with his ammunition crates and his occasionally macabre correspondence, Otto Schlüter's business continued, at reconstructed offices on the old site. His mother recovered slowly from her severe injuries. Then, on Easter Sunday, 1957, a second bomb exploded. But this time, Schlüter made sure that no information reached the press.

He, his wife, and children were visiting with his mother in Braunlage in the Harz Mountains. Just before the family sat down to a festive breakfast, the youngest daughter asked if she could look outside to see if the Easter bunny was at the door.

They all went, and although they saw no bunny, the diversion saved their lives.

As they looked for the bunny, the breakfast table exploded; honey, jam jars, sugar bowls, and Easter eggs whirled through the air; the windows burst into tiny fragments, and in seconds the room was a smoking heap of rubble.

Considering his Hamburg experience, Schlüter was frantic to avoid publicity; he invented some half-credible story, paid for the damage, and the police and public never knew there was a bombing.

He returned to Hamburg after the holidays, and continued his business as usual.

Schlüter was beyond reproach. Every one of his transac-

Sporting rifles from Otto Schlüter's bombed-out weapons depot: intended for hunting elephants or colonial soldiers in Africa.

Photo: Collection Bernt Engelmann

tions was legal, executed in the heart of the business district, far from the obscurity of a dark alley. His business practices were not unlike those of other merchants, bankers, and brokers in the international port of Hamburg, and he always had the proper license.

The following was a typical transaction: In the summer of 1955, a few months after the outbreak of the Algerian uprising, he completed a $75,000 order for hunting rifles, signal pistols, and ammunition for the president of the Chamber of Commerce in Tripoli. The rifles were actually Mauser carbines, but after the bayonet holders and sights had been removed, the weapons, according to international codes, were unfit for military purposes. They were now considered sports or hunting equipment, and so it was with the ammunition—where, of course, no changes were necessary. How the customer used the merchandise was not Schlüter's affair. Nor was it any of his concern that the Libyan royal family was of Algerian descent and sympathized strongly with the Algerian rebels, sending them gifts of sports and hunting equipment.

In another transaction in 1955, in September, the Tunisian Chief of Rural Police ordered a thousand 9mm pistols. There was nothing unusual about automatic pistols, machine guns, and armored self-propelled guns being urgently needed somewhere just at the time Schlüter was obtaining a special license for their import from Finland. Why not cooperate? After all, his clients were not obsure smugglers with a cellar bar for an office. Like their bank, Martin Friedburg & Company, their offices were in the heart of the city.

Under such circumstances, Otto Schlüter had every reason to defend himself against the inflammatory stories about him in German newspapers. From then on, every paper that called Schlüter a profiteer doing dirty business with rebels was sued immediately.

He had no less than thirty-six lawsuits pending, and he won every one, receiving payments of considerable amounts from German and foreign newspapers. The walls of his rather modest office displayed an increasing number of trophies won in battle: apologies and corrections, each beautifully framed and mounted.

It seemed no one could attack Otto Schlüter—except the assassins. On the morning of June 3, they struck again.

The night before, a black Citroën—bearing a French tag —occupied by two men, drove several times through the suburban area in Hamburg-Eppendorf, where the Schlüters lived. Soon afterward, a sand-colored Opel stopped at a vantage point favorable for observing Schlüter's house. Two men were in the car. They switched off the lights, and waited. Then a third vehicle arrived: a silver-gray Porsche with a young girl behind the wheel. Two men were in the back seat. This car went slowly past the house, rounded the next corner, and stopped. The two men left, and the girl remained behind the wheel, keeping the engine running.

The two men from the Porsche walked slowly back to the house where Schlüter's black Mercedes was parked. One of them carried a heavy black briefcase. He looked back toward the Opel, whose lights flashed on and off.

During the next six minutes nothing happened—at least nothing that could have been noticed by an observer. Then the two men walked slowly back to the Porsche. They got in, and the girl drove off, back along the street they had come through, signaled by flashing the headlights, and disappeared.

At that moment the Opel left its observation point, and drove off.

On the opposite end of the quiet street, the parked Citroën started up and disappeared down another street.

The following morning, June 3, 1957, at 8:12 A.M. Otto Schlüter left his residence—Loogestieg 10. With him were his sixty-two-year-old mother, Kathi Schlüter, and his seven-year-old daughter. They walked together to his Mercedes. At 8:13 A.M. Schlüter helped his mother into the car. She sat in the seat next to the driver, as always. Then he waved good-bye to his daughter, who turned to go to school, got in behind the wheel, and started the engine.

Otto the Strange One:
at his twenty-fifth court victory over the press.

At 8:14 A.M. the engine purred. Schlüter put the car in gear, and stepped on the accelerator. The heavy car began to move—it rolled for two yards. A tremendous explosion ripped the car to pieces—a jet of flame shot into the air, the roof flew off, and Schlüter's mother, fatally injured, was thrown into the street.

His daughter, Ingeborg, who had just waved happily after the car, was hurt by metal and glass fragments. Covered with blood and paralyzed from shock, she stood on the curb. Only one person was unhurt—Otto Schlüter.

About a year later, he again escaped almost certain death. On the Hamburg-Lübeck expressway, his left front tire exploded from a well-aimed shot from another car. Schlüter's car, driven at seventy miles per hour, somersaulted and landed on its roof. He climbed from the wreck unharmed.

Because of Schlüter's repeated narrow escapes, a rumor circulated among his colleagues that Colonel Mercier—Chief of the Special French Police for the prevention of supplies to Algeria—had forbidden further attempts on his life. Every bomb used against the apparently invincible merchant would be irresponsible waste. Whatever the reason, no more assassination attempts were made.

Schlüter continued his business transactions, even after his mother's death, and, as usual, obtained all necessary official documents. The Hamburg Criminal Police, despite their efforts, could find no trace of the assassins, and hope for their capture was abandoned.

Seidenschnur had expected no less, and he could not understand my interest in these aborted killings so far in the past.

Even Schlüter expressed considerable doubt that I would find a connection between the Puchert assassination and the attempts on his own life.

He had met Puchert casually. Immediately after his arrival in Germany, the man from Tangier had paid him a visit and wanted to buy explosives.

But Schlüter did not want to be involved. His merchandise

The risks of a million-dollar deal:
above, Puchert's Mercedes in Frankfurt, and *below,*
Schlüter's Mercedes in Hamburg after auto-bomb explosions.
Photos: Collection Bernt Engelmann; dpa, Frankfurt

was confined to weapons and ammunition—the sale of explosives was controlled far too rigidly.

No business association developed. But shortly before Puchert's death he had again visited Schlüter. And Schlüter, normally talkative, became reserved when I tried to question him about this visit.

As much as I tried, Schlüter did not want to talk about his last meeting with Captain Morris.

"Let dead men rest," he said.

Dead men—was this just a phrase, or had the plural some particular significance?

"Did you know the other one also?"

Schlüter hesitated.

"Well, I met Léopold once, at the house of Friedburg the banker—that is all. It was long ago, and I was somewhat surprised when Puchert mentioned him."

He would say no more.

I quickly wrote down the names on the margin of an old newspaper I had found on the table. And when I left, I asked Schlüter if I could take it. It was part of an old news report about the bombing on his street. Schlüter had another copy in his files, and had no objection to my taking it.

For the rest of the day I tried to remember where I had heard the name "Léopold." The second name, Friedburg, was no doubt the owner of the bank that played such an active part in the weapons business.

But who was Léopold?

Then, at the dinner table, I suddenly remembered. Two years ago, in Geneva, a man had been killed under mysterious circumstances. Staying at an exclusive hotel, he had taken the elevator down to the lobby, which was crowded with the usual international set, and there he did something considered shocking in an elegant Swiss hotel: he collapsed and died. The result of the inquiry was even more embarrassing: The deceased was an important buyer for the Algerian rebels, and was well known in the international weapons trade as a buyer of explosives. He had not died a natural death. Somebody did not like him or his profession, and had noiselessly shot him with a dart dipped in curare, a lethal poison used by South American Indians on their arrows. There was no trace of the murderer. Apart from the dead man's business and name, Marcel Léopold, nothing was known about him.

I quickly finished my dinner, and called Schlüter. When he answered, I apologized for the late call and told him frankly what had occupied my mind since I last talked to him. He laughed.

"Of course, I meant Marcel Léopold," he said, "but we don't have to talk about it over the phone. If you have nothing better to do, come over and have a beer with us."

I accepted the invitation, and half an hour later arrived at the home of a man who had escaped four attempts on his life. Ingeborg, who had recovered from her injuries, set the table; his son, Otto, brought beer and brandy; and Mrs. Schlüter insisted that we have something to eat. She appeared young, healthy, and contented, showing no trace of her horrifying experiences during recent months. A black ribbon and a small bunch of flowers at a framed photograph of Schlüter's mother were the only reminders of the violent past.

The entire atmosphere was so relaxed and friendly that I found it difficult to direct the conversation to the reason for my trip. Only once did he touch on the subject of weapons traffic. Mrs. Schlüter said: "My husband does nothing that isn't legal. He stays away from all corrupt business."

And her husband added: "It's absurd to assume that the attempts on my life were connected with the Algerian uprising. I have never furnished them anything, not even one bullet. Either it was revenge by those who thought my reasonable prices would affect their business or I was chosen as a scapegoat to intimidate the German arms merchants. Also, there is no connection with Puchert's murder. I'm sure he was killed by his own people."

I did not agree with this theory, which I had heard before from Seidenschnur.

I enjoyed seeing Schlüter's normal family life, which was

quite different from what sensational-minded newspapers would
have us believe: One would expect an armed bodyguard leaning
on the doorframe, and the "big boss," who had escaped death
four times, to be watching the street nervously through a slit
in the curtains. And of course there would be mysterious telephone calls to Trieste, Tangier, Barcelona, and Rome.

Only when I thanked Schlüter at the door for a lovely
evening did something occur to satisfy the imagination of the
yellow-journal readers. When my host unlocked the front door,
his coat opened just wide enough to expose the shaft of the gun
he carried in a shoulder holster.

Back in my hotel room, I recalled again everything that had
happened that day. Had my trip to Hamburg been worthwhile?

I went through my sparse notes, threw away some scraps
of paper, and then found the old newspaper I had taken from
Schlüter's office. Just as I was about to throw it away, I noticed
the following article: "Children playing on Loogestieg found a
number of steel pellets. The possibility of a connection with
yesterday's attempt on the life of Otto Schlüter, the weapons
dealer, is not supported by the police. However, the steel pellets
have been sent to the explosives expert at the Federal Investigations Bureau in Wiesbaden for further study."

Now I was sure my trip to Hamburg had been worthwhile.
The bombings of Frankfurt and Hamburg were closely connected.

Weeks later I learned that a series of international crimes
were being committed.

On Sunday, July 5, 1959, in one of Rome's quiet resi-
dential streets, a bomb exploded under a parked car.

Playing children had touched off the fuse when their leather
football rolled under the car. A six-year-old boy was killed, and
six other children were critically injured.

The day after the bombing I flew to Rome. In the afternoon I met the owner of the bombed car at his residence.

He was Algerian.

He had overslept on Sunday, or he would have driven off long before the children began their football game. He would not have gone far: perhaps three or four yards.

His name was Tajeb Bularuff.

His friends called him Mabrouk, "The Lucky One." He held the same position in Rome as that of the Algerian Ait Ahcène—shot to death on the diplomatic race strip in Bonn—chief of an unofficial Algerian Mission, a "shadow ambassador."

In Italy, as in West Germany, everything indicated that weapons smuggling to North Africa was opposed by the same means: bombs and bursts of gunfire.

The Italian police were as unsuccessful in finding the criminals as their German colleagues had been in Frankfurt and Hamburg. And the Italian officers were a few degrees cooler. It was impossible to obtain any information from them about the bombing.

I was dependent on my own observations and conclusions and on the information Mabrouk generously provided. The results were meager, but I made progress: The bomb planted in Rome had been of the same explosive force as the bombs against Schlüter and Puchert—this could be determined quite accurately by the impact of the explosion. A mechanical fuse had been used, touched off by the football that rolled under the car. And finally, I knew that the children had been injured by steel pellets —I bought one from one of the boys for thirty cents.

One more piece of information I gathered in Rome: Mabrouk remembered that in Rabat, in November, 1958, a Frenchman sympathizing with the Algerian cause had been killed by an auto bomb of the same type. The Rabat police, Mabrouk said, had announced shortly after the bombing that the group responsible were known to them through a remarkable discovery.

So I flew from Rome to Rabat, not directly, but via Barcelona. Ferhat Abbas, the senior chief of the Algerian revolution—later, President of the Algerian Parliament—lived there, acting as President of the Tunisian Government-in-Exile. A tele-

The lucky one:
Mabrouk Bularuff, the near-victim of the Rome
auto bomb, tells his story.

Photo: Petra Engelmann, Hamburg

gram from Mabrouk enabled me to obtain a dinner invitation to Abbas's house. Of course, bombs and smuggling were banned from the conversation.

In the morning, I traveled to Morocco with a short letter in my pocket from the friendly exiled President.

"It will be useful to you in Morocco," he said.

The letter was addressed to Sidi Mohammed ben Yussuf el Alaoui, the then Sultan of Morocco and father of the future king.

The Sultan received me in private audience in a wonderfully cool hall of his snow-white, one-story palace in Rabat. It was absolutely quiet. The windows were covered by heavy drapes, keeping out the scorching July heat. Beautiful chandeliers provided a soft light. King Mohammed V, Sultan of Morocco, wore Arabian clothes, white and cool. He was very friendly. Again, bombings and smuggling were taboo. He asked a few polite questions about German-Moroccan relations. I answered respectfully. The audience lasted about ten minutes. Then I was again outside in the scorching summer heat, dressed, according to protocol, in a dark suit, and thought sadly of the cool summer in Germany with all its rainy days and its cool draft beer.

The next morning, dressed in navy blue, I visited Minister Lachsaoui, responsible for national safety. Wearing dark glasses and a white open-neck sportshirt, he sat behind his desk between two fans, and the blinds were tightly shut. My connection with the Sultan proved useful. Lachsaoui sacrificed one of his fans for my comfort. Journalists generally are unaccustomed to courtesy in North Africa.

The Minister made no other attempt to assist me. I tried weakly to direct the conversation toward smuggling and bombs, but failed pitifully. We had two glasses of hot mint tea together, and I took my leave. As I reached the door, he asked me to collect two letters his secretary had prepared; they would perhaps be useful.

The first of these provided access to the files on the murder of Auguste Thuveny.

Following Moroccan liberation, the people elected Thuveny—a liberal Frenchman—their Attorney General. His first, self-assigned task was to wipe out the bomb terrorists. These were members of a French underground organization, a forerunner of the OAS (Secret Army Organization, *Organisation de l'Armée Secrète*), who kept Morocco in constant fear by their desperate attempts to reverse history and to restore the days of colonialism.

Auguste Thuveny failed in his undertaking. He was assassinated on Sunday, November 23, 1958. A bomb exploded beneath his car in front of his house, just as he drove off. The Attorney General was torn by numerous steel pellets, and died instantly.

The Minister's second letter took me far overland: for lack of better transportation, in an old bus that had been parked in the sun. At the incredible maximum speed of about twenty miles an hour, the vehicle groaned over endless dusty roads. I was fortunate to get a seat by the window, because the bus was crowded with women transporting their livestock.

About seven hours later, toward evening, I reached my destination, the residence of a high state official.

I handed over my letter of introduction, was received with warmth and dignity, and shown to a sparsely furnished but very clean guest room.

The evening passed over a seemingly endless dinner: giant-sized puff paste, cinnamon-sprinkled pies filled with pigeon meat and raisins, followed by enormous mutton roasts, then couscous with chicken, an array of sweet pastry, fruit, and tea.

Shortly before midnight I retired to my room, without premonition of what I would find.

When I opened the door, I thought at first that I was entering the wrong room; but then I recognized my suitcase, and realized I had a visitor. On the only chair in the room, dimly lit by a solitary weak electric light bulb, sat a young man in police uniform. In opening the door, I apparently woke him, and now he jumped from his chair.

Beside him on a wobbly table was a carefully wrapped and tied shoebox. The sleepy young police officer saluted, then quietly started to unwrap it. The box contained a second, smaller one, carefully wrapped in newspaper. He unwrapped that too, saluted again, and retreated respectfully.

Before me on the table was a small metal box, about 5 inches long, 3 inches high, and 3½ inches wide. On its front was a small projection with green nylon wire spiraled around it.

Suddenly it dawned on me. This was a perfectly intact auto bomb.

The police officer who had watched my face stepped forward and handed me a slightly creased slip of paper. In a crude hand and in unsophisticated French was the statement that the enclosed device had recently been found and confiscated in the luggage of a man under investigation as a member of an extremist right-wing French terrorist organization. The powder had been removed, and also about 350 small steel pellets, of which one was enclosed as a sample. The device in its present condition would be harmless. I could dismantle it at my convenience, and take photographs.

The device was not quite so harmless as my Moroccan associates thought. In its "present condition," it could blow the tired police officer and myself through the thin walls of the house.

The oversight is understandable. The Moroccans had removed the 350 pellets (with a diameter of about ¼ inch) and the powder surrounding them from the hollow in the middle of the device. With that, they had assumed the bomb would be converted into a harmless metal box.

But the eager police had overlooked the fact that the walls of the shell itself were hollow, and still contained enough explosive to blow more than the small box apart. Furthermore, the fuse had not been disarmed, and was composed of two highly explosive detonator capsules.

I was greatly relieved when the box was rewrapped and put back in its shoe carton, and the officer saluted and disappeared.

But before this was done, I measured the box, weighed it, took all sorts of samples, and photographed everything as best I could.

I took the results back to Germany. My suspicions soon were confirmed. The attacks against Schlüter, Puchert, Bularuff, and Thuveny had all been carried out with bombs of the same construction and composition, within three years and in four different places: Hamburg, Frankfurt, Rome, and Rabat. The bombs had been attached to the individual cars as shown in the illustration.

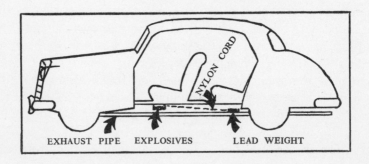

EXHAUST PIPE   EXPLOSIVES   LEAD WEIGHT

When the car began to move (or a football bounced under it), the lead weight fell off the exhaust pipe, thereby pulling at the nylon cord. . . .

Four months after Georg Puchert's assassination, I had solved the mystery of the auto bombs, and had sound evidence that the bombings at Hamburg and Frankfurt were only links in a chain of similar actions.

No less, but also no more.

It would still be a long time before I discovered the names of the assassins and obtained enough evidence to prove their guilt. A thorough investigation of their motives, interrelations,

Auto bomb:
three stages.

Photos:

Collection Bernt Engelmann

and also the environments was necessary—theirs and that of their victims.

Both groups lived in the same world of secret wars and international weapons smuggling.

And no one would be better suited and more willing to introduce me into this twilight world than Hans Joachim Seidenschnur, the man I had met in his Bonn Liaison Office of Belgian Armaments Manufacturers two days after Puchert's death, and who, during the unforgettable dinner, had told me of Puchert's acquaintance with Schlüter.

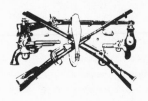

MINING EXPLOSIVES
FOR MONROVIA

HANS JOACHIN SEIDENSCHNUR, the elegant and worldly manager, displayed slight impatience at my concern about the bombings; after all, such accidents were not too important.

They were annoying, but unavoidable—and not very disturbing to a smoothly run and flourishing business. And the high death rate among the weapons dealers, he accepted, coolly and unperturbedly, as an inevitable risk; only the market was affected, and prices would go up. Seidenschnur saw no reason to shed any tears for Puchert, whom he preferred to call by his nickname, Captain Morris; still, he often spoke highly of him during our various conversations.

When we had a "little snack" at the Bad Godesberg Maternus Restaurant, commencing with fresh Helgoland lobster, Seidenschnur remarked that Captain Morris had actually stimulated the international and especially the German market, and he deserved to be highly commended for this accomplishment.

I was still trying to interpret this statement, when Seidenschnur, nibbling on his lobster tail, continued in a sorrowful voice, ". . . but then Puchert lost his nerve, and unfortunately he made some very stupid mistakes."

The nature of these "stupid mistakes" he explained during the rest of the meal.

Georg Puchert did not confine his business connections strictly to his friend Seidenschnur and his Bonn Liaison Office, but made contacts elsewhere, with Otto Schlüter and several other Hamburg weapons dealers.

Captain Morris appeared in the international port of Hamburg almost every week. Feeling secure, he was careless enough to make a bet for twelve bottles of the choice and expensive Chivas Regal whisky with a Danish business associate, J. J. Petersen, an exporter who will be described later.

He bet that he could rent a suite in the exclusive Hotel Atlantic on Hamburg's Aussenalster, the favorite meeting place for foreign officials and the upper echelon of German society, using his real name, full address, and, most important, his actual profession.

Puchert won the bet.

He appeared in the hotel's register as Georg Puchert, alias Captain Morris; residing in Tangier, Morocco; temporary address: Frankfurt am Main, Lindenstrasse 3; profession: Weapons Dealer.

This unusual entry caused neither consternation nor even concern at the distinguished hotel. The bar of the Atlantic, accustomed to extravagant and unusual people, sold a record quantity of twelve bottles of Chivas Regal that evening; and the excellent reputation and quality of this peak product of Scotch whisky distillers was again proved by the fact that the principal consumer, Georg Puchert, displayed no hangover symptoms the morning after.

That day a high-spirited Puchert entered Otto Schlüter's private office. He planned to gain the support of the gunsmith and his excellent organization for the Algerian cause.

Following a proved strategy, he explained the enormous demand of his North African friends.

Of course, Schlüter was interested.

This was a chance any merchant would want to investigate.

But Otto the Strange One was careful—he suspected a catch. Why would Puchert approach him? With financial resources of such magnitude at his disposal, he should do his buying in the posh offices of the big armaments syndicates.

Otto Schlüter was not too enthusiastic, and Puchert explained the particular difficulties of transactions with North Africa.

The quiet Captain Morris became unusually talkative. He had hoped to enlist Otto Schlüter's sympathy for the heroic fight of the Algerians, particularly since Schlüter's life had been threatened so often by their common enemy.

But the gunsmith did not appreciate mixing politics with business.

The difficult supply situation of Wilaya 5 might be of interest to Schlüter as a businessman, but Puchert's ideals or those of the Moslems in North Africa did not in the least concern him. Of course, he wanted to do business, and Puchert's prices were attractive. But Schlüter would only accept orders for which he could obtain export and transit licenses from the authorities in Frankfurt. He did not understand why Puchert could not get these documents. But here was the main obstacle and also the reason for offering skyrocketing prices. East Algeria, bordering Tunisia and Libya, could easily be supplied with weapons. The embassies or consulates of the Arabian brother states from the Gulf of Sidra to the Persian Gulf were more than willing to legalize all documents necessary for the import of weapons via Cairo, Beirut, Tripoli, or Tunis. From these points transportation continued overland, on the wide coastal road along Alexandria to Tunis without harassment by the French Navy or Air Force. From this coastal road, many secret branches continued westward to Algeria. But the *West* Algerian war zone, Wilaya 5, which was Captain Morris's responsibility, could be supplied only through Morocco. This kingdom had won independence in 1956. Sultan Mohammed V had returned from exile, and again resided in his white palace in Rabat, and the country was now represented by ambassadors in all important capitals. But strong

French garrisons still controlled the strategic points, in addition to the presence of American and Spanish troops. French fighter-bombers and reconnaissance planes controlled the Algerian border, and French high-powered speedboats and destroyers patrolled the coastal areas. Together with an army of secret agents of the French security police, this powerful force secured strict obedience to a clause contained in the Moroccan-French Treaty, which confined the procurement of weapons to France alone, and limited their quantity strictly to Morocco's own requirements.

Therefore the Moroccans, despite their sympathy with the Algerian cause, were unable to assist—officially. Weapons had to be smuggled in as before, but controls were now applied by Moroccan customs officers, and sometimes they were prepared to look the other way.

None of this either concerned or moved Otto Schlüter.

He wanted to know whether he could count on regular orders complete with import licenses for an unrestricted consignee, including an official declaration that reexportation of the dangerous cargo was not intended. Only with such documents would an export permit be issued by German authorities, and without this—no business.

But Puchert replied there might be a way. He knew a young lady, the friend of an influential Liberian merchant with dark skin and very enlightened mind. The merchant, besides other gifts, had given his blonde girl friend one-quarter ownership in a small export-import agency. A controlling interest he retained for himself, the balance going to the favorite Finance Minister's nephew. This flourishing Liberian enterprise was situated in Monrovia, capital and commercial metropolis of Africa's oldest native republic.

Puchert proposed that some merchandise might now be directed to Monrovia. There would be no difficulty, and all the necessary documents could be provided. En route, the ships would stop briefly at the port of Casablanca; some innocent merchandise could be found for this Moroccan port. And it could be predicted that, without serious inconvenience for the consignee in Monrovia, the entire cargo could disappear in Casablanca—by mistake or theft.

Otto Schlüter remained unmoved. Maneuvers were not his concern. Only the orders that could be expected from the Liberian agency, and for which all official documents could be obtained, aroused his interest.

Captain Morris knew exactly what he wanted: The first order was for sporting ammunition—7.92mm steel jacketed bullets with a lead center. This type of bullet is used to hunt elephants and rhinos, and coincidentally is no different from infantry ammunition for the 98K Mauser carbine.

Puchert foresaw an elephant and rhino population of huge proportions, and predicted a hunting fever—his estimate was for an order of approximately 1½ million rounds.

But his predictions went further: There was a possibility that Monrovia's small port could be blocked in the future by shipwrecks, and this could seriously endanger the country's economy. Quick action would then be necessary, and it would be of great advantage to have explosives available for immediate blasting operations. Monrovia seemed to exaggerate its needs, because Puchert mentioned a demand for 200 tons of explosives.

Schlüter was not very impressed. He was glad to learn of Liberia's great demand for sporting ammunition. This was in his field. Explosives, however, were not part of his merchandise, and he wanted no involvement in this end of the business.

Otto the Strange One had some association with Martin Friedburg & Company bank, whose premises were nearby and who were not only engaged in the usual banking business, but also acted as agents for weapons transactions.

Unfortunately, this was the same firm that previously had been approached by Seidenschnur. And it was Seidenschnur's luck that just at this time, October, 1958, Captain Morris had received information about the anonymous letters to the various governments. Puchert's rage, of course, was directed against his former friend and contact, Seidenschnur, whom he rightly suspected to be the author. And it did happen that the sale of 200 tons of TNT took place, as planned, in Drammen, Norway, but with one slight alteration: Seidenschnur had been left out.

This was a particularly telling blow for Seidenschnur, because he had already chartered a ship to load the cargo. The ship was ready, and would cost thousands of dollars in demurrage charges. In the meantime, the Danish freighter *Granita,* chartered by Puchert, steamed toward Casablanca, carrying an initial part-shipment of 40 tons of TNT in its hold. The bill of lading was for "Mining Explosives for the Removal of Shipwrecks in the Port of Monrovia, Republic of Liberia."

But the betrayed Seidenschnur was quick to get his revenge. The *Granita* did not reach her destination despite Puchert's precautions. She was stopped by a French destroyer near the south Portuguese coast, and, in violation of international law and treaties, was forced into the French naval base of Mers-el-Kébir near Oran, Algeria, where the entire cargo was unloaded and confiscated.

The TNT reached Algeria's shores faster than Captain Morris had anticipated. However, it would not be used for its intended purpose: to blow up French barricades and fortifications, but was used instead by French combat engineers against the Algerians. And it would not be too improbable to assume that the auto bomb that blew Captain Morris to pieces in Frankfurt contained a tiny fraction of the 40 tons of TNT.

Of course, there was nothing coincidental about the French destroyer lurking off the Portuguese coast. The betrayer of the TNT transport was never made known because the French Intelligence Service not only paid a high price for information leading to the capture of such transports but also handled such affairs with the strictest discretion. The name of the informer is a highly speculative matter.

In spite of the satisfaction Seidenschnur must have obtained through his part in the ill-fated TNT transport and Puchert's subsequent loss, he wrote him a nasty letter in the name of the Bonn Liaison Office of Belgian Armaments Manufacturers, a letter without salutation, which deserves to be read carefully:

Subject: Your TNT order for Morocco, dated July 8.

We received the above order to supply 40 tons TNT for a total amount of $100,000 CIF destination.

The merchandise was obtained by us in collaboration with several groups in Denmark; we chartered a Norwegian freighter through a German agency, negotiated with the insurance company, and finally ordered the freighter to the loading port of Drammen to receive the cargo on October 14, 1958.

The ship waited there until October 24, 1958, accumulating a daily demurrage in the amount of 45 pounds sterling (approximately $125).

Today we have been informed by the suppliers that execution of the planned transaction was stopped by your representative Georg Puchert, alias "Morris," by giving the manufacturer the impression that we were unable to accept responsibility for transportation of the merchandise.

By this action and through your fault, you deliberately destroyed a business transaction, initiated by us, for which all necessary licenses and papers had been obtained.

We therefore hold you responsible for all expenses incurred thus far, that is, a total amount of $8,800. The loss of profit resulting from your default is as follows:

Sale price		$100,000
Purchase price	$14,500	
Transportation and insurance	8,000	
Unloading	10,000	
	$32,500	32,500
Loss of Profit		$ 67,500

As stated in our contract of July 10, 1958, 50 percent of this amount, that is, $33,750, plus expenses in the amount of $8,800, plus $2,000 advance payment to Mr. Puchert, totaling $44,550 represent our share.

We expect payment by November 30, 1958. If we should not receive this amount by that time, we shall be forced to take legal action, and will inform your Embassy.

Bonn Liaison Office
of Belgian Armaments Manufacturers
(*signed*) SEIDENSCHNUR, Managing Director

This outcry of a suffering merchant was addressed to Puchert's firm in Tangier—Astramar, S.A.—an enterprise established for the purpose of organizing the arms supply to Algeria's Wilaya 5.

When Seidenschnur handed me a copy of this letter, I was, first of all, surprised by the extraordinarily high profit margin in dealings in TNT: At a purchase price of $14,500, the customer was supposed to pay $100,000—a net profit of over 200 percent.

Then I noticed the high expenses, for instance the unloading: $10,000 for forty tons! The amount most certainly included some payoffs to Casablanca's customs officials. I was not astonished to learn that Seidenschnur had already spent $8,800 while preparing the transaction. I thought of numerous meals he must have had with shipowners, agents, and insurance brokers; of the trips, telegrams, and long-distance phone calls, and the bottles of champagne emptied in anticipation of a profitable deal. When I read the letter again at a later time, I noticed several other interesting points:

Monrovia and the threatening shipwrecks were not mentioned, but simply explosives for Morocco.

Also, the merchandise was not declared as mining explosives but as TNT, despite the fact that trinitrotoluene is used mainly for the purposes of war.

I noticed the embarrassing reference to the fifty-fifty profit-sharing clause in the agreement between Seidenschnur and Puchert, alias Morris, and further the advancement payment of

$2,000. Both these points were of particular significance when connected with the intent of the final paragraph: If Puchert should not pay, the Algerians responsible for the administration of the war funds would be informed that their chief buyer was sharing in the enormous profits made by his supplier.

When I questioned my talkative friend again about this point, he nodded his head solemnly, ordered another half bottle of Piper Heidsieck of a vintage highly recommended by connoisseurs, and said in a genuinely mournful voice, "When the date came due for Puchert to pay his debt and I had received no reply, I forwarded a copy of my letter, via an Arabian Embassy in Bonn, to the Algerian Government-in-Exile in Tunis."

He gave me a meaningful glance, and when I did not react, he continued: "This has presumably contributed to the Algerians wanting to settle their account with Puchert."

The champagne was served. Seidenschnur took a little sip, then emptied his glass in one swallow and had it refilled, paying the proud bar waiter all sorts of polite little compliments.

The leisurely meal gave me ample opportunity to reflect on Seidenschnur's exceptionally gentle description of the assassination, and his tactful references to the likely motives for Puchert's murder and assumed identity of the assassins.

But Seidenschnur's efforts were in vain.

I knew that the tracks he pointed out so emphatically were misleading because I already knew who was behind the scene of the auto bombings.

But I did not understand another significant hint in the letter. It mentioned "several groups in Denmark" that had worked in collaboration with Seidenschnur—that had also been deprived of their well-earned profit.

Who were the people in these "groups?"

During the weeks and months after Puchert's assassination, a piece at a time was added to the puzzle, and fairly soon I understood the last mysterious hint in Seidenschnur's letter.

It appeared that the groups that allegedly assisted Seidenschnur's Liaison Office in the explosives procurement had, at the same time, also been helpful to Captain Morris, not only in

Drammen, Norway, where the TNT had been bought, but also in Africa, to be exact, in Tangier. There, these same groups had obtained a 50 percent interest in Astramar S.A. and consequently also had a 50 percent share in the profits from the order placed by the ominous Liberian firm.

These groups were small. In fact, they consisted of only one gentleman who acted in the TNT deal as the Astramar partner, as sales executive, and broker.

This versatile businessman was the Danish exporter J. J. Petersen, and, since August, 1958, the owner of a 50 percent interest in Puchert's company. It was he who received the original letter from the indignant Seidenschnur addressed to Astramar. But Petersen paid no attention to it.

His interest in the company, in the TNT deal, and in further transactions with Puchert and Seidenschnur had already faded. He then severed all connections with North Africa, but remained faithful to his business: weapons. The world was wide, and weapons were also needed elsewhere, for example, the Middle East.

Therefore not until later, when I extended my investigation to the really big international weapons business, would I meet J. J. Petersen.

At the time of my "snacks" with the effusive Seidenschnur, Petersen had retired completely from the Algerian activity and severed all connections with his partners. The reason for the sudden change of mind of an otherwise tough and determined businessman was a message delivered to him shortly after the *Granita* confiscation. The messenger was scarface Pedro on a mission assigned by Jean-Paul Mesmer, alias Colonel Mercier.

Unlike Puchert, Petersen's first contact with the threats of the assassins was enough to make him withdraw from the Algerian business. Consequently, he survived his partner and would continue his weapons trade, but not with France's enemies. Petersen developed a preference for customers whose adversaries were less effective than Colonel Mercier's Intelligence agency.

Here I shall drop the deterrents that persuaded Petersen

from his profits, and investigate the much stronger motives that caused an honorable exporter of Danish agricultural products to turn his talents and energy to weapons.

J. J. Petersen's promotion from a dealer in cheeses to a merchant of weapons is a unique example of a man in the prime of life lured from the righteous path—from the export of eggs, butter, and cheese to machine guns, mortars, and explosives.

For this reason, I am neglecting the business aspects in favor of the private, intimate sphere of Petersen's weapons business. And for the same reason a name has been changed—to J. J. Petersen.

HOW TO BECOME
A WEAPONS MERCHANT

PETERSEN'S CONVERSION OCCURRED during one mild summer night.

An entire series of events was caused by an unconcealed yawn.

It was about 11:00 P.M. in the days when the lights of the metropolis were slowly extinguished and all Copenhagen went to bed.

But the Petersens were not at home in their beautiful red brick house in Tömmerup, but in the Casino de la Méditerranée at Nice.

They were vacationing, enjoying the world and its pleasures. Their son and daughter, both in senior high school, had gone to a dance on a café terrace close to the casino entrance on the Promenade des Anglais, the magnificent street along the shore. The lively sound of the dance orchestra could be heard through the wide-open windows of the casino. But in the gambling rooms the atmosphere was subdued. The croupiers' monotone announcements and the clicking of the ivory roulette balls were the only sounds.

Petersen sat at one of the roulette tables; his stakes were

low despite, or perhaps because of, his being well off. He had lost about $20, and had reached a degree of petulance befitting a Copenhagen cheese merchant. But when he quickly won back $10, he considered himself to be a daredevil.

Mrs. Petersen yawned. She was more than bored.

"Darling," said Petersen to his wife, who was sitting at a table behind him, sipping a champagne cocktail whose main ingredient was orange juice, "I've won! Let's order a bottle of Cliquot!"

It should be noted that Petersen's father once had spent an Easter week in Paris. According to his reports of the event, as far as he had passed them on to his son and heir, a bottle of Cliquot had been the crowning peak of the evening. Petersen wanted to carry on his father's tradition and, at the same time, do something to please his wife.

But Mrs. Petersen refused brusquely.

"I've had enough of this," she said, "and you should have too. All that good money you've been squandering. I can't stand it any longer! I'm going to bed!"

With this she stood up, curtly refusing her husband's gallant offer to accompany her to the nearby hotel, and, with this action, assumed responsibility for at least one successful revolt in Central America, and a bloodily suppressed uprising in Kurdistan. Because just after she had left the casino, her maltreated husband gave into a desire to break the bank. He multiplied his thus far modest stakes, became more and more daring, put $5, even $15 on one particular number, and, surprisingly enough, won.

At about 1:00 A.M. he had accumulated more than $2,500 and it seemed his luck would continue.

At 2:30 A.M. he had won nearly $4,500, a reputation, and many new friends. The waiters and croupiers whispered to the interested players and spectators that the white-haired, tanned, lucky gentleman at Table 3 was a "fabulously wealthy brewery owner from Denmark," with an interest in Sweden's match industry, owning vast stretches of forests extending to the polar circle, a seagoing yacht custom-made from mahogany, and a mansion at Cap d'Antibes.

The new friends that flocked around Petersen came from a variety of backgrounds. There was a somewhat persistent elderly gentleman who was trying to get Petersen interested in an absolutely foolproof gambling system that would multiply his considerable winnings; an ancient lady who, mentioning the emperors of Russia as her royal ancestors, was prepared to part with some of her precious crown jewels just to please Petersen—for some remuneration, of course; several young and not so young inventors; owners of gold mines and oil fields; trustees of patent rights; and candidates for exotic royal thrones.

All wanted J. J. Petersen to be a partner in their projects, requiring only minor investments to get them started. And there was the grandniece of the Russian heiress mentioned above, seventeen years old, aristocratic, pale complexioned, with large, soft doe eyes. And there was the nineteen-year-old fiancée of a gold-mine proprietor. She was long-legged, affectionate, and—unlike the Russian grandniece—suntanned, and she could speak English, a distinct advantage, because Petersen spoke English fluently. It was quite natural for Petersen to turn his attention to the gold-miner's fiancée—since she had not made any clumsy attempts to extract his winnings. On the contrary, she nearly refused—slightly indignantly—the bets he placed for her on his own lucky numbers.

By about 3:00 A.M. Petersen's winnings had increased only slightly, but his fondness for the suntanned girl was mounting steadily.

They left the roulette table and ordered champagne at the bar. Petersen finally had his bottle of Cliquot, and made a date with his new friend, Gaby, feeling like an adventurous young buck.

After a long farewell kiss, Gaby whispered that she would leave her fiancée and live only for him. And Gaby kept her word.

They became inseparable during the following days and weeks, at the beginning spending long nights together at the casino, and later—after the Petersen children returned to school in Copenhagen and Mrs. Petersen joined another Danish cheese merchant and his wife on a two-week Mediterranean cruise—during all their free hours.

It turned out to be a long, relaxing, and very expensive vacation for Petersen. His luck at the roulette table did not last, and in order to maintain his reputation as a wealthy industrialist he repeatedly wired his bank in Copenhagen for the immediate transfer of large amounts of money.

When Mrs. Petersen returned from her cruise, and his happy days with Gaby ended, Petersen had spent not only his original travel funds and his winnings at the roulette tables, but also an additional $850.

Gaby had accumulated a brand-new, luxurious wardrobe, some jewelry, a small sports car, and an apartment in a fashionable house on the Promenade des Anglais. It was rented in Petersen's name, and paid in advance for the next six months.

From this point on, I shall refer to Gaby also as Gaby Petersen, though it was Mrs. Petersen to the concierge, the shopkeepers, and the mailman.

During the following months Gaby Petersen was visited at irregular intervals by her "husband," who was kept in Copenhagen most of the time by his demanding and ever-increasing business. The original Mrs. Petersen, however, was pleased to note the extraordinary expansion of the cheese business, and made allowances for her husband's numerous business trips.

Petersen's journeys did not take him straight to Nice, which had excellent direct flight connections with Copenhagen. If the increase in business were to seem plausible, Petersen would have to make considerable detours and stopovers. He established branches in Paris, Zurich, Munich, Vienna, and Rome, ordered letterheads indicating all these branches of his export agency in fine, embossed type, increased his enterprises by adding subsidiaries in Hamburg and Trieste, and soon became known as Denmark's busiest agent for butter, egg, and cheese exports.

All Petersen's offices were staffed by young ladies. To ensure variety, he selected blondes, brunettes, and redheads of the most subtle varieties to represent his expanding empire. But all had common characteristics: long-legged, full-chested, affectionate, under twenty, and fluent in English. The dairy exports did not occupy them full time, and therefore they took courses in modeling, or earned pocket money posing as photographers' models. Petersen's employees could be seen on calendars, in magazines, and sometimes in fashionable society journals. They modeled brief pajamas and bikinis, and sometimes just themselves.

Always on call for the export business, they lived in small modern apartments that served as local headquarters for the Petersen dairy enterprise. The name on all these apartments, whether in Munich, Vienna, Zurich, Hamburg, Paris, Rome, or Trieste, was Petersen, and the young ladies had no objections if they were addressed by business people, porters, or mailmen as Frau, Madame, or Signora Petersen. To simplify matters, it should be remembered that the legal Mrs. Petersen resided in Copenhagen and Gaby Petersen lived in Nice. Other Mrs. Petersens shall be known as III, IV, V, and so on.

It is easy to see that Petersen's fortune—acquired partly by inheritance and partly through his work—could not withstand the combined onslaught of so many wives and business branches. His original enterprise was quite profitable, and expansion to other cities yielded a new customer here and there, particularly since his local representatives were pretty and unattached. Still, Petersen could easily foresee impending disaster. A few more months, and nothing would be left for his not-too-far-off old age. J. J. Petersen was in his sixties.

Petersen returned to the Riviera—to Nice, the site of his rebirth.

Gaby celebrated her twentieth birthday.

Petersen—who had spent thousands for the recent Christmas holidays—alighted from a taxi and, enjoying the mild sunshine, walked toward the apartment house where Gaby lived. He boarded the elevator, giving the tiny package in his hand a doubtful glance: It contained a flawless diamond of one and a half carats, for which he paid a $75 deposit. The price was $450, half of what it should have been. Would Gaby be satisfied with the gift?

Wearing a white bikini, stretched out in an easy chair on her wind-protected balcony, she seemed grateful and most eager to please. Petersen thoroughly enjoyed the attention it brought him, but he could not completely ignore a foreboding of its limited duration. And he could have saved $75! Gaby Petersen would have been just as satisfied with a box of candy, and would still have showered him with affection. She had a guilty conscience, and an uncomfortable feeling that her old friend and sponsor would find out why.

Not even Petersen could be naïve enough to assume that a girl lavishly endowed by nature and well provided for would lead a monastic life on the sunny Mediterranean shores during her benefactor's prolonged absence.

Her foreboding proved correct.

That evening Petersen noticed the peculiar black cigarettes Gaby smoked, her habit of taking her coffee black and very sweet, a newspaper printed in Arabic in a dresser drawer, and in the kitchen, between some aprons, he discovered a soiled navy-blue, turtleneck sweater of the sort sailors wear. And it smelled of tar and tobacco. Gaby could see disaster looming, and with the courage obtained only through despair, she tried to prevent it.

During recent weeks, Mahmout, boatswain on the *Ville d'Oran,* and forty years younger than Petersen, badgered her to persuade her rich Danish friend with the international connections to add a lucrative product to his line. She had always resisted, but now she saw that Mahmout's plan was her only chance to dispel Petersen's dawning doubts about her faithfulness—at least for the duration of her secret interlude with the Algerian sailor.

"My brother-in-law Mahmout paid me a visit," she said. "My sister's husband, your brother-in-law too, so to speak. He wanted to make you a proposition that could yield enormous profits."

The suspicion left Petersen's eyes, and he seemed interested. She continued: "Mahmout is Algerian, and an officer in the French Merchant Navy. He is also one of the leaders in the revolt over there."

She nodded toward the Mediterranean, sparkling in the warm January sun. By 1956, everyone knew about the war in Algeria, even Petersen, who took no interest in politics.

"Tell me about the proposition," Petersen said, impatient.

He took the bait! thought Gaby, greatly relieved. And she eagerly gave her aging lover a detailed description of Mahmout's plan: The rebels had practically unlimited funds—voluntary contributions and forced dues—extracted from their Arabian brothers in Morocco, Tunisia, Libya, Egypt, Syria, and Jordan, subsidies from Iraq, the Lebanon, Yemen, Saudi Arabia, and the oil sheikdoms on the Persian Gulf. They had millions to spend, but they were in desperate need of weapons and ammunition, military boots, canned food, and cigarettes—in short, everything required by an army at war.

"We have good canned bacon and ham in Denmark," Petersen remarked thoughtfully, "and also beer and aquavit."

"They're forbidden to Moslems," chided Gaby.

Petersen was willing to learn.

He listened attentively while Gaby outlined the North African rebels' needs, as explained by Mahmout; the prices they would pay, and instructions on how to get the shipments through.

Petersen calculated and added long columns of figures well into the night, and when he had finished, said, as though to himself: Even a fraction of this business will save me!

Gaby had to tear him away from his figures, but the next morning his thoughts again were filled with the fabulous prospects, and he said: "Where can I find this Algerian? Introduce me to him immediately!"

By coincidence the *Villa d'Oran* was expected at Marseilles that very day. Gaby volunteered to meet the ship, and promised to return with her brother-in-law. Petersen wanted to accompany her, but she suggested it was inadvisable for security reasons. He agreed, and patiently waited until the following morning, when they arrived looking fatigued. With his arm congenially around Gaby's slender hips, the rebel leader demanded breakfast, which she skillfully prepared with amazing speed. Petersen had overcome his original mistrust; he was no longer interested in whether Gaby had a married sister and consequently a brother-in-law. The essential point was that Mahmout had arrived and was ready to discuss business.

However, there remained a minor technical difficulty: Mahmout spoke little English, and Petersen's French was poor. But Gaby proved to be a capable interpreter, and very soon negotiations were under way.

By the afternoon, the first transaction was agreed upon: Mahmout, acting for the Algerian Liberation Army, placed an order with Petersen for 10,000 pairs of boots from United States Army stocks; 1,000 pairs of binoculars of Japanese origin; 150,-000 cans of corned beef; 3,000 signal pistols and ammunition; 18,500 sheath knives of a type worn by the Hitler Youth during the Third Reich, and, the highlight of this initial order—a high-powered speedboat from World War II.

Such an offer required many lengthy long-distance calls, the mobilization of old and the creation of new contacts, and all of Petersen's mercantile talents. He bargained and beat down the suppliers, and if everything went as planned, he expected to make a clear profit of about $43,000 in the transaction.

But the best feature was that the entire shipment, plus transportation and insurance costs, would be paid for before unloading in the port of Tunis by a letter of credit drawn on Swiss banks. Moreover, Mahmout was prepared to make an advance payment of $14,500 in cash.

Gaby escorted Mahmout back to Marseilles, and returned the following morning, again looking sleepy but carrying an old brown suitcase filled with money.

The overjoyed Petersen asked no questions.

Gaby received 10 percent of the money as a gift from Petersen before he returned to Copenhagen to explore further sources of supply.

During the next fifteen months Petersen developed into one of the most important suppliers for the Algerian forces. He procured everything: automatic pistols from Finland, carbines from West Germany and Bulgaria, explosives and ammunition from Norway and Sweden, pistols from Italy, and powdered eggs from China.

Those ramifications of his business that were pleasant proved useful as well. When his long-legged girls saw a chance to make some easy money, they eagerly offered their services, and often found the most amazing, hard-to-obtain merchandise for amazingly low prices. Petersen rewarded such zealousness with hard cash, and he was always generous.

For example, Mrs. Petersen III, an ash-blonde Italian who lived hear the Via Veneto, was given a contract with a film company, and earned enough money in one evening to purchase a villa. She just happened to remember, at the right moment, having heard from a gentleman—a relationship that was the same as Gaby's was to Mahmout—that in Cinecitta, an Italian movie town, the warehouses held German antiaircraft guns once used to make a war movie, and they were rusting away. Several long-distance calls, hard bargaining with the warehouse custodian, a bill of sale notarized after midnight by a lawyer friend of Mrs. Petersen III, the skill of two Italian mechanics, and the efficiency of an American antirust preparation provided the French Air Force in Algeria with an unexpected antiaircraft barrage. The French suffered heavy losses, which boosted the fighting spirit of the Algerian guerrillas, who had so far been helplessly exposed to air attacks. It also caused the Russians and

Americans to take the Algerian revolution seriously, and notably influenced the debate on Algeria brought before the full United Nations Assembly in New York.

During this historic night, in addition to the 30 German 8.8cm antiaircraft guns referred to, Petersen purchased 46 British and German 37mm pom-pom guns; and 40 Italian and German 2cm guns. He paid $15,000 for the lot. The mechanics were paid another $5,000 for the overhaul, and he then sold the merchandise, FOB Trieste, for $685,000.

As usual with a good business deal, everyone was satisfied: The Algerian buyer was praised by his boss; the mechanics could buy a small workshop of their own; the film company had more storage space in their warehouse; the custodian bought himself a cottage; Mrs. Petersen III obtained the film contract for at least one minor movie role, and later, after she had secured a multimillion-dollar transaction for antiaircraft ammunition with the help of two elderly senators and a retired artillery officer, bought her dream villa on the shores of Lago Maggiore.

The rewards:
dealer's villa on Lago Maggiore.

Photo: Collection Bernt Engelmann

J. J. Petersen made a clear profit of more than $1,000,000 on this Italian antiaircraft weapons deal, and remembers the transaction fondly.

When Pedro visited him on a gray morning in the fall of 1958 in Copenhagen with the blunt demand to retire from the weapons business with Algeria, he could oblige immediately without fearing for his security in his golden years.

He severed his connections only with Algeria, Puchert, Seidenschnur, and the banker Martin Friedburg. His branch offices were staffed with the many Mrs. Petersens he maintained, and before long, through his considerable experience in the international weapons business, he made new contacts with the world's weapons dealers. The inactivity during the winter of 1958 was therefore only a brief interlude during which Petersen could devote some time to two responsibilities he had sadly neglected—the export of cheese and the original Mrs. Petersen.

When I met Petersen about one year later, he had been through this phase of retirement. We had arranged an appointment in the hotel Vier Jahreszeiten in Hamburg, where he and his wife had taken a suite.

I was introduced to Mrs. Petersen IX. She was a pretty doe-eyed Dane with black hair, meeting the Petersen specifications exactly: long-legged, full-chested, under twenty, and fluent in English. Unlike the other Mrs. Petersens—II through VIII—this one, like the original, lived in Copenhagen, but was obviously not involved in the arms trade; she had not the faintest notion about the source of Petersen's income. I found this out when I asked Petersen about the Kurdistan business, and whether they had now converted to modern automatic weapons.

But the vigorous exporter blushed all over, signaling frantically that the weapons trade was not to be discussed in the presence of Mrs. Petersen IX. She was not supposed to know. I complied with his wish, but it was difficult to maintain a polite conversation with him when the subject of common interest was not to be mentioned.

Mrs. Petersen IX solved the problem in a simple way. She wanted to dance, so we departed for the Riverside Club.

Fortunately, we met a young Danish couple, casual acquaintances of Petersen: The wife, who had a sprained ankle, remained with us but she knew nothing of German or English. Her husband, a passionate dancer, took Mrs. Petersen IX to the dance floor again and again, and I could talk shop with Petersen. Though we were interrupted many times, the result of our conversation was satisfactory.

Incidentally, Petersen had not the slightest idea that he was being interviewed by a reporter, because the obliging Seidenschnur's recommendation introduced me as the "man engaged to settle the Puchert estate."

Holding 50 percent of Puchert's Astramar shares, Petersen naturally would claim it out of Puchert's estate, and so he showed me the sunniest side of his character. Without restraint he spoke of the good old times before Puchert's appearance in the European weapons market, when practically everything bearing some resemblance to war matériel could be sold to the Algerians at a profit of 150 to 200 percent.

He spoke enthusiastically of his first transaction with United States surplus boots, and of corned beef not fit to pass European health controls but, nevertheless, suitable for half-starved guerrillas on the northern edge of the Sahara Desert or in the rugged valleys of Aurès. And when he mentioned the coup with the antiaircraft guns, his eyes sparkled.

He was less pleased with his deceased friend and partner. Of course, why abuse him now?—but Captain Morris had been unfair to conceal from his good old Astramar partner where and how the multimillion-dollar profits had been invested. And then to depart without revealing the wonderful secret! Petersen was genuinely shocked.

Listening to him, I got the impression that Puchert had requested to be murdered for the purpose of cheating Petersen out of his share in Astramar.

But when I casually mentioned that Marina Puchert had not yet seen a penny of her father's fortune and that neither she nor the FLN had been able to find the money, he pricked up his ears. His pale-blue eyes, so far directed constantly toward the dance floor, intently watching every movement of Mrs. Petersen IX, focused on me for the first time with genuine interest.

"So you are trying to find the Astramar money here in Hamburg," he said slowly. "I should have thought of it myself. But how are you going to persuade Dr. Krüger to reveal his information? He is very cunning, and, being a lawyer, he knows how to stay within the law."

He looked at me questioningly.

It did not seem the right moment to reveal my profession and my real intentions, and I did not want to show my ignorance of the man he just mentioned. I said quite truthfully: "Personally I'm not interested in the Astramar millions. I'm only trying to shed some light on the reasons for Puchert's assassination."

He did not reply, but when we parted about an hour later, he whispered: "If you find a trace of the money Puchert hid, let me know; it won't be to your disadvantage. And try your luck with Krüger."

It was not difficult to locate Dr. Krüger.

But before I took up this new lead, I made some inquiries. First I asked Otto Schlüter.

"Dr. Krüger!" Otto the Strange One exclaimed. "Of course I know him. His offices are located in Brandstwiete, and he also owns the import-export agency, Brock & Schnars, which has a license to sell weapons. By the way, during Puchert's last visit he mentioned an appointment with his lawyer. And when I asked him the name of his lawyer, he laughed and said, 'Dr. Krüger, of course.' But if you want to know more about Dr. Krüger, you should take a trip to Bad Segeberg and see Mr. Springer."

With this information, I took leave of Otto Schlüter, and that same afternoon I went to Bad Segeberg.

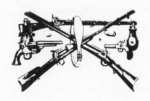

THE CASE OF
THE COOKIE TINS

BAD SEGEBERG IS A DISTRICT CAPITAL and health resort in Schleswig-Holstein in northern Germany with a population of only 15,000. Apart from a district court, a spa hotel, and a beautiful cathedral, there is an open-air theater at the base of the 100-yard-high Kalkberg where every year the Karl May Festival is held. Here honorable Holstein citizens are converted into yelling bloodthirsty Indians, screaming for the scalps of pale-faces and performing war dances to the uninhibited joy of old and young. Or the sheriff shoots them from their Holstein horses, which have been upgraded to mustangs for the occasion.

This generally satisfies the average Segeberg citizen's demand for the romantics of war. But it did not satisfy Ernst Wilhelm Springer, who lived with his family in a small cottage in the suburbs. I visited the Springers on a rainy afternoon. I was kindly received and was served coffee and home-baked cake. Their well-behaved boys helped Mrs. Springer set the table, placed floral-patterned cups and saucers on the hand-embroidered tablecloth, and produced the family's best cigarette case, ashtray, and matchbox holder, all engraved with Arabian symbols.

A few more interesting objects in the room brought a touch of the Orient to the otherwise bourgeois home. In front of the writing desk used by the head of the house, a genuine Oriental prayer mat was spread out. A Damascene dagger, heavily embossed in silver, served as a letter opener, and on the bookshelves five camels stretched their wood-carved, haughty heads.

I learned something about Springer when I discovered, directly below the wood-carved caravan, the titles in his library. There were *Mein Kampf*, a *Manual for the Use of Arms*, a *Handbook for Prospective Merchants*, and a variety of travel and war stories about North Africa, and also the *Reibert*, the notorious drill manual used in all German barracks squares by army instructors. "The soldier must wash his hands and face, also his neck and upper torso," flashed through my mind, and I could just visualize how Springer would have surprised those willing Arabian soldiers with such an order, especially after he had just made them crawl on their stomachs over the hot desert sand.

When the master of the house arrived, my assumptions were confirmed: Ernst Wilhelm Springer, in his mid-thirties, tall, and broad-shouldered, made no attempt to conceal his former SS membership or his association with the Arabian Legionnaires whom he drilled during World War II. Nor did he hide his continuing faith in the ideas of the Führer. He was also loyal to the Arabs, and he believed in weapons. But his former occupation now had been converted to the commercial side.

"What are your needs?" my host inquired amicably. "Perhaps you want machine guns? Or tanks? I can offer tiger tanks, never used, well preserved. But you can have also any other war matériel."

I explained that I had no demand for weapons, especially not for mothproofed tigers. I was only curious—professionally curious!

But my comment did not lessen his garrulity, nor did it diminish his enthusiasm about my visit, particularly when I told

"Preserved tiger" for sale:
Ernst Wilhelm Springer, weapons dealer from Bad Segeberg
and pillar of the Schleswig–Holstein, extreme right.

Photo: Petra Engelmann, Hamburg

him that I was on the track of Puchert's assassins and his estate.

"In this matter you can count on my full support," he said. "And, generally, I have nothing to hide. I am a public figure."

I was speechless.

Actually, Springer had exaggerated only slightly. He was one of the founders of the *Sozialistischen Reichspartei* (Socialist Reichs Party, SRP), had been a member of the provincial government as a representative for the party—the repository for Hitler's faithful and now dissatisfied subjects—and was, together with his friend Remer,* considered the best fighting orator of the Extreme Right in the northern area of West Germany.

However, I was not interested in the politician Springer, whose career had been rudely interrupted by his party being declared illegal, but in the successful merchant. I directed our conversation quickly back to the starting point.

"Did you have any business connections with Georg Puchert?" I inquired.

My host answered somewhat evasively, so it appeared: "You know the case of the cookie tins, which, you will of course remember, had upset our relationship? I really had to restrain myself then."

I nodded solemnly, despite the fact that I was completely ignorant in the "case of the cookie tins."

Since Puchert had obviously been involved, and the transaction had been interrupted, I said haphazardly, "This must have been a heavy blow to you—and to Wilaya 5!"

I realized immediately that my reply had been just right, because now whatever remained of Springer's reserve vanished. During the next thirty minutes, over coffee and cake, he told me all about the case of the cookie tins.

---

* Otto Ernst Remer was the former commander of the Berlin Guard Battalion. For his loyalty to Hitler on July 20, 1944, when he assisted very actively in suppressing the uprising, he was promoted to major general. After 1945, he turned, together with Ernst Wilhelm Springer, to politics and the weapons trade.

There was a factory in Luxembourg that was making excellent automatic pistols, just what the guerrillas of Wilaya 5 wanted. But the directors of the company were prohibited from selling to enemies of France. And there was the accursed transportation problem.

In Frankfurt, Georg Puchert had considered the matter from all angles, and finally found a solution. And for this, he had obtained the necessary assistance.

There was a young lady, an unemployed actress, whom we shall call by her first name only: Corinna.

Corinna's acting abilities may have been questionable, but definitely not her appearance. She possessed that animal magnetism so effective with men in the prime of life. Outfitted with a brand-new wardrobe that accentuated her fine points, and a chic sports car, Corinna employed her charms with a determined purpose, and conquered, in accordance with Puchert's orders, one of the directors of the Luxembourg arms factory.

The first part of her assignment was accomplished within one week.

It took another week to find out that not even the directors had the authority to dispose unrestrictedly of their dangerous products.

During the third week she and her new director friend discovered a way out of their dilemma.

Like any other factory, the Luxembourg plant's products were not all of superior quality, and some were rejects. A number of automatic pistol barrels and locks were apt to be faulty, and would land on the scrap pile. The more strictly quality control was carried out, the more rejects were collected, and when a quantity had accumulated, they were sent to a steelwork to be melted and the metal reused.

In the following weeks quality control was applied more and more stringently. About a thousand barrels and locks more than usual wandered to the scrap pile every month—or, to be exact, to a stockroom well protected against corroding and destructive weather effects.

Fortunately, no suspicions were aroused at the factory. A buyer was quickly located who paid a very agreeable price for the "better rejects," as this merchandise was called. For single assorted parts of an automatic pistol the buyer paid the full price of a brand-new assembled weapon of first-class quality bearing the stamp of the quality-control department. The assembled automatic pistol parts looked exactly like a well-approved, brand-new weapon.

In this way, 1,000 and later 1,200 automatic pistols left the Luxembourg plant every week through the "back door," the scrap pile. They were collected in a garage on the outskirts of town and later could have been found again in the trunk of a sports car with a German tag passing the German-Luxembourg border quite often and—because of the heavy traffic—during weekends, holidays, and at the beginning and end of the summer vacation period. They were well camouflaged and packed in convenient quantities, but nobody ever tried to search the car because a very attractive young lady was behind the wheel.

The next stage was a garage near Trier at Corinna's base of operations, a beautiful small apartment, just big enough to accommodate her and the Luxembourg weapons supplier for some intimate hours.

An ordinary minibus, which had proved to be of excellent service to Puchert in a previous transaction, transported the merchandise to Frankfurt once a week, and the pistols reached their last station on German soil at the Rhine-Main airport. Packed in tins of the type that are used for the airtight storage of cookies, and declared as machine spare parts, the cookie tins piled up in the airline's storage rooms, awaiting air transport to Casablanca. Much machinery and many vehicles of German origin are used in Casablanca, and the continuous stream of spare parts imported by a large Casablanca workshop aroused no suspicion. And because such spare parts are classified as valuable and urgent goods, air transportation seemed justified.

The authorities might have noticed that the exporter specified a peculiar route his merchandise was to take: Frankfurt-Brussels-Casablanca. But all exporters have their peculiarities, mostly the result of disconcerting experiences; an especially urgent shipment could have been loaded onto the wrong plane. In any case, the freight was not to be routed through France, but to be transferred to Brussels for the direct flight to Morocco.

Because the customer's demands are usually met, especially in the air-freight business, everything went according to schedule for months, until one day, after more than 10,000 automatic pistols were already in use in Algeria, a small accident occurred that was to shatter a smooth business—literally shatter it, because one of the cookie tins slipped out of the grip of a worker at the Brussels airport during its transfer to the Casablanca plane. The tin dropped about fifteen feet and hit the concrete with great force, thereby spilling its heavy contents all over the runway. A small misfortune, unavoidable despite the greatest care. It would have been of no further consequence had the freight supervisor who came hurriedly to the scene not been a war veteran and recognized a gun barrel when he saw one.

This is how the case of the cookie tins came to an end. The freight supervisor notified the Belgian airport police, who contacted their colleagues in Frankfurt. The Frankfurt police determined the origin of the "spare parts," and informed the Luxembourg security police. And so not only the stream of automatic pistols to the Algerian war zone ran dry, but also Corinna's source of steady pocket money.

Though she dropped out of her director friend's life, unscathed, he was in serious trouble. Over coffee and cake Springer, urged on by my cautious questions, had been generous with the details of the cookie-tin incident, but his own role remained obscure.

"Were you directly involved?" I asked.

"Only indirectly," answered my host darkly. "I had a financial interest in it."

The extent of his financial interest remained vague, and I decided to drop it.

Much later, when I checked Springer's version of the cookie tins and found it verified in all essential points, I realized the reasons for his reluctance to discuss his own role in the affair.

At that time Springer was in serious difficulty, and I hadn't (and still haven't) any inclination to add to his troubles. Despite his bragging, he was only a little wheel in the big international arms business. Behind it were men no authority would dare investigate. They will be discussed later. Unlike Springer, these tycoons enjoy a high standing in society regardless of the fact that everybody knows or at least guesses the source of their wealth. These men are dignitaries and, because of the influence they undoubtedly have on world politics, are treated deferentially.

Ernst Wilhelm Springer once made world politics, and even then only involuntarily and by a chain of coincidences, for which he had to pay dearly.

During the initial phase of the North African uprising, the former SS drill instructor was approached by a group of influential Arabs living in Bonn who asked him to procure, perhaps together with "reliable" friends, weapons for the guerrillas fighting against the French.

Springer agreed without hesitation—first because he sympathized with the Arab cause, and second because he expected not only a reward from Allah but also large profits.

He chose for his partner a man with whom he had maintained political contacts during the postwar period and whose rigid National-Socialist views were unassailable, the Hamburg lawyer Dr. Fritz Peter Krüger.

The Arabs welcomed his choice. Although Krüger had not been their comrade-in-arms during the last war, he had, nevertheless, published with SS support a book entitled *The Jews in England*, and he had assisted the *Reichssicherheitshauptant* (SS Intelligence Service), Department VI–Foreign Countries, in the establishment of a small branch network in the Middle East. The Arab customers also welcomed the fact that a fully accredited lawyer, who was on extremely good terms with the respective authorities and politicians, was a member of the team. Dr. Krüger was a defeated Christian-Democrat candidate for the Bundestag.

Their operation progressed satisfactorily. Springer discovered through old SS connections an excellent source of supply: The Czechoslovakian government-controlled export agency, Omnipol, in Prague, offered old German weapons at very favorable prices. Agreement was reached for a part shipment in the amount of $375,000, consisting of Mauser carbines 98K, MG42 machine guns, several bazookas, and the appropriate ammunition. Several brand-new Russian bazookas were also included in the Czech offer.

The Arabian customers would take all, but because the Czech prices were ridiculously low, Springer placed a firm order only on condition that the merchandise would have to pass inspection at the Czech border before acceptance.

Krüger traveled to Bratislava to inspect the weapons supplied by Communist Czechoslovakia for the North African rebels.

After a short and seemingly satisfactory stay in Bratislava, Krüger reported that he had counted and sampled the merchandise, that it was in first-class condition, and that it had been properly crated for overseas shipment and loaded onto railroad cars.

Relying on this final positive inspection, the Arabs released payment, and the crates were dispatched in sealed railroad cars from Bratislava to the small Yugoslav port of Peroj on the Adriatic Sea between Trieste and Pola.

The two gentlemen, Springer and Krüger, also traveled to Peroj, planning to supervise personally the loading of the crates onto a waiting freighter chartered especially for this purpose. Springer was to accompany the dangerous merchandise to its destination, Tangier. Krüger was to return to Hamburg to conclude the financial aspects, mainly calculating their considerable profits. But things took an unexpected turn.

The Yugoslav authorities were suspicious of the shipment,

and as soon as the crates were unloaded from the railroad cars they were confiscated and stored in a government warehouse. Also confiscated were the passports of the fiercely protesting German gentlemen, who were ordered to remain in town and take lodgings in the only available inn. Until final clearance, they could consider themselves under house arrest.

It was several weeks before an Arab diplomat could effect the release of the crates. In the meantime, the originally chartered freighter had left Peroj; and a new ship had to be found. All this was expensive. Krüger finally returned to Hamburg, relieved to escape both the suspicious Yugoslavs and his dismayed partner, who remained in Peroj for further instructions.

After several anxious days, Springer received his orders. A freighter had been chartered and would arrive in Peroj within one week to load the cargo, but would sail to a different destination, with Springer on board. Tangier was now too dangerous, because the affair in Peroj had alarmed the French Intelligence Service.

Springer carried out his orders. After the freighter had arrived and the cargo was on board, he exchanged his room at the Peroj inn for the second mate's cabin, grudgingly assigned to him.

It was not until they had reached the high seas that Springer was informed of their destination. The ship did not head west toward Tangier or Casablanca, but due east to Latakia on the Syrian coast. The journey was uneventful, but Springer counted the hours until he could hand over the troublesome cargo to his Arab friends, and depart for Germany. On a beautiful sunny morning the small ship reached the port of Latakia.

Springer was astonished to find a large crowd assembled on the shore. There were festive decorations; flags fluttered merrily in the breeze; and, to top it all, the Syrian Navy Artillery fired a salute.

The gala reception, however, was not meant for Springer,

nor was it meant for the weapons destined for their comrades in faroff North Africa. The festivities were in honor of a flotilla of Russian Navy vessels on a friendship mission to Latakia— traveling in the wake of the little freighter.

The coincidence was to have far-reaching consequences.

At the time, Springer had other worries. He waited feverishly for the consignees of the shipment, and when an Egyptian emissary finally arrived, Springer greeted him like a beloved friend.

The Egyptian remained aloof, and explained that he had instructions to open every crate and inspect its contents.

Springer was offended, "Suit yourself," he said. He was unconcerned, because his partner had carefully inspected the merchandise in Bratislava and verified its perfect condition. The crates had been sealed and the seals were intact. With all these precautions, what could possibly go wrong?

Quite a lot.

To begin with, Springer, the Egyptian, and the captain entered the hold, found the seal of the first crate intact, opened the crate, inspected its contents, and stopped, thunder-struck.

The crate contained carbines, thickly greased and wrapped in oilcloth, but apart from their brand-new leather straps, the rifles were all junk. Every one was completely useless. On most of them the locks were missing; on others, the gunsights and firing pins had been forcibly removed.

The weapons in the other crates were even worse. The plastic butts of several machine guns had been broken off and replaced by makeshift pieces of wood tied to the barrels with piano wire; the locks were missing or had been destroyed.

The antitank guns were ancient Russian models with rusty iron wheels, with barrels cracked from misfiring—in short, the whole shipment was completely useless for military purposes and could only be considered scrap metal. Only the Russian bazookas, the extra bonus, were brand new and intact.

The Egyptian, of course, refused to accept the shipment, and because the captain wanted to get under way again, it was agreed to transfer the cargo onto small boats that would remain in port to await further orders. The Egyptian had the few bazooka crates unloaded on land. There they were discovered by one of the many spies, and that very same evening an interesting, politically important intelligence was sold in the Café Metropol, headquarters for such information: "Brand-new Russian and Czech weapons were unloaded today in Latakia. The alleged friendship visit of the Russian warships were an escort for the weapons."

Naturally, this important information was bought also by the local CIA agent, and one hour later it was decoded by a conscientious Navy lieutenant in the code room on board the flagship of the United States Sixth Fleet and classified "Urgent."

The Navy lieutenant then called the officer on duty. "We have just now decoded a radio message from Latakia which the admiral should see immediately."

What actually happened in the office of the commander of the United States Mediterranean Fleet during the night can only be guessed. The admiral was in possession of a spy's report about a very tense situation in the Lebanon (the Lebanon border was only a few nautical miles from Latakia); trouble was brewing in the Middle East, and the Russian weapons shipment would put the United States on the alert. The admiral would regard the situation as extremely critical, and contact Washington immediately.

On the same night, while sleep evaded the furious Springer, all shore leave granted to the personnel of the United States Sixth Fleet was canceled; they were put on alert; and not much later the fleet steamed toward the Syrian-Lebanon border.

This incident was to be the final push for United States intervention in the so-called Lebanon crisis; soon afterward the United States Marines landed in Tripoli.

But before these world-shattering actions took place, their involuntary instigator, Springer, poorer in hope, faith, and money, had departed from the Middle East and returned home.

On the way he found sufficient time for speculation: What

World crisis created in Segeberg:
Marines from United States Sixth Fleet in Mediterranean
intervene in Lebanon.

Photo: dpa, Frankfurt

would the consequences have been had he landed with his crates
of scrap metal in Tangier instead of Syria? The reception by his
Arabian friends would not have been generous. They would
certainly have brought charges against him, at best, imprisoned
him until his partner had returned their money. And, Springer
justly assumed, his cheated employers and he could have waited
a very long time.

Springer also recalled the "inspection" by Krüger in Bratislava. Not even the most ignorant layman could have mistaken
the scrap metal in the crates for usable weapons. Had the crates
been opened at all? Or had Omnipol paid some bribe money
for Krüger's ignorance? Hard currency in the amount of $375,-
000 for scrap not worth even one-twentieth of that amount;
Prague must have made some sacrifices!

In any case, the Egyptians and Syrians had the scrap metal; Krüger and the Czechs had the money; and the Algerians and Springer had nothing.

During my return trip from Bad Segeberg, I gave Springer's account of his partnership with Dr. Krüger some more thought. I felt that the story was essentially true. This was later confirmed by an Arab diplomat, at that time ambassador in Bonn and later the representative of his country in Moscow. And because this diplomat was one of those who had suffered a financial loss in this transaction, he should have been well informed.

But how was it possible, I asked myself, that Georg Puchert, who was employed by the same groups that had financed and lost the deal with the Czech weapons crates, established business connections with the lawyer Krüger? Captain Morris had arrived in Germany *after* this affair. Had he not been warned?

How could he select this lawyer whose performance in Bratislava had such catastrophic consequences to act as his adviser in new, important weapons deals?

I could not solve this puzzle, not even after a personal meeting with Krüger, whom I visited in his city office.

How in the world is it possible, I thought, while climbing the worn stairs in the office building at Brandstwiete 2, that a member of the honorable Hamburg legal fraternity can be a weapons smuggler without offending his sensitive colleagues?

The question was answered instantly.

Not the lawyer Dr. Fritz Peter Krüger was dealing in weapons, but the businessman Fritz Peter Krüger, owner of the old, established export-import agency Brock & Schnars, Inc., at Brandstwiete 2, a company licensed in Hamburg to sell weapons.

The fortunate circumstances of having a law office and a weapons export agency housed under one roof often had been to Krüger's advantage. For example, he is not compelled to give information to the police and the district attorney. The contents of Krüger's safe have the benefit of legal immunity, and how can a distinction be made between files pertaining to legal cases or weapons deals if they are kept under lock and key at all times?

Nevertheless, Krüger did not attempt to conceal his activities in the international weapons business.

"In my opinion, lying is not a character weakness but stupidity," he said.

He attached great importance, however, to justifying his behavior—so contradictory to common practices of his profession—through an "idealism," or, to be exact, "ideologies."

"All my life I have studied the Jewish question," his reasoning began. And then he explained that his part in the Czech weapons sale was not "common greed" but the "common battle against the Jews," and he had joined ranks with the Arab Nationalists for this good cause since World War II.

Regardless, the "common battle against the Jews" had helped him to some tidy profits. Besides his law business and the import-export agency, he had acquired a stone quarry and a ranch on the outskirts of Hamburg after the German collapse.

Regarding the common cause with the Arab Nationalists, one of their leaders, the then Moroccan ambassador in Bonn, Abdelkebir El Fassi, said, when I asked him about Dr. Krüger: "He is barred from our country—unfortunately, our trust in him was betrayed."

The strange lawyer was quite willing to explain his racial theories, overlooking completely the fact that his Arab friends are also members of the Semitic race, but he suddenly became extremely reserved when I asked for some precise definition of his relation with Puchert.

"I cannot give you any information on this subject," he said. "This comes under my professional discretion." I replied that this matter possibly would not so much concern the lawyer as it would the exporter and that the licensed export of weapons was not bound to any professional discretion.

But Krüger remained mute. Perhaps he thought of the assassins. Among his acquaintances there had recently been some unexplained explosions. Schlüter, who had his store and office only a few streets away, had escaped several attempts on his life, and Puchert, Krüger's customer and business associate, was dead. Springer, Krüger's former partner, found a bomb under his car several weeks after our meeting. Springer had been warned by a mysterious caller.

And still another weapons dealer who was acquainted with Krüger was visited by the assassins in those days: the businessman from Munich, Dr. Beissner, former SD and SS leader, partner of Springer, Remer, and Krüger in several covert weapons deals with North Africa and the Middle East. Despite a warrant for Dr. Beissner's arrest as a war criminal, the police allowed him to live undisturbed in Schwabing, Munich, in a comfortable apartment in Blütenstrasse. He could almost be considered a prominent citizen by virtue of his membership in a group—meeting regularly in a tavern—that included influential Bavarian politicians, ex-ministers, industrialists, and members of the aristocracy. These connections were valuable for Beissner's weapons business.

Only the assassins were unimpressed with Dr. Beissner. When he started his car in front of his house, a bomb exploded under the vehicle. Beissner, badly injured, was rushed to the hospital. He recovered after many operations and long treatment. Released from the hospital, he and his wife, who was known in the business as "blonde Alice," hurriedly left Munich for North Africa, where Beissner reopened a manufacturers' representative's agency. He had worked in this field before, during the years after Germany's collapse.

Schlüter—Puchert—Springer—Beissner.

But the name of Krüger was missing on the list of the assassins, and so was that of Seidenschnur. Was this a coincidence, lack of information, or was there a purpose behind it? It would be some time before I could question a really pertinent source—the assassins themselves.

I had not planned to write about my meeting with members

of the Red Hand. My intention was to limit myself to the weapons merchants, and not to write about those people viciously engaged in a search-and-destroy action against them. But then the scourge of the weapons merchants solved this problem for me in a very simple manner—the Red Hand began to deal in machine guns and explosives themselves!

LITTLE NAPOLEON

THE ORGANIZATION RESPONSIBLE for the assassination attempts on Schlüter, Beissner, Springer, and many other weapons merchants in Germany and other countries was never identified. In fact, there was not even a thorough investigation. The bold and fatal shooting of the Algerian "shadow" ambassador in Bonn, Dr. Ait Ahcène, was added to the police files of unsolved murders and soon forgotten by the press. The Puchert case, however, was still being investigated by the Frankfurt police, who were not likely to give up.

This was due partly to the considerable public indignation aroused by the Frankfurt West End bombing. Only seconds before the explosion, a group of children on their way to school had passed the ill-fated vehicle and, as in the Rome explosion, could have been killed or injured; also, numerous Trade Fair visitors were staying in that area, and many had sent reports of the crime to their home countries. Moreover, the crime was not investigated by "political" police, but was the responsibility of the Homicide Squad. These officers, with a wealth of experience in major crimes, were not in the least concerned with the possibility of antagonizing France, but were searching for murderers, and to feel restricted in the execution of their duty by political considerations was out of the question. This attitude was reinforced by the investigating team's leader, Frankfurt's District Attorney Heinz Wolf.

Wolf was a striking contradiction to the image of the typical German law officer leafing through dry files, aloof from the public. Like his colleagues in the United States, he collaborated with the police, personally supervised the efficient execution of investigations, and kept the public informed through press conferences.

On April 16, 1959, Wolf revealed to the public that Puchert's assassination was the work of the Red Hand and that this secret organization was most probably working in collaboration with and, what is more, on orders from France's Counterintelligence Service. He then issued warrants for the arrest of three men suspected of being connected with Puchert's murder—the same three men mentioned several times in this book: "scarface" Pedro, "killer" Viari, and "little Napoléon" Durieux.

Pedro was the man who had delivered the warning to Puchert to intimidate him, who had some encounters with Captain Morris's business partners, and who had continued to live unmolested in Bonn after the shooting of Ait Ahcène in front of the Tunisian Embassy. And he did not hesitate to brag about his unerring aim.

Viari, the former French police officer, Puchert had first met in Casablanca, and later in Bonn. Here is his description as stated on the warrant for his arrest: "Jean Viari, age 37, 6′1″, athletic build, black hair, dark eyes, slight resemblance to Elvis Presley."

And Durieux, the baby face, was Number Three on Colonel Mercier's team of active agents.

At the time of Wolf's press conference, I had collected some material on Durieux, who had been seen before Puchert's assassination and during the attack on Ait Ahcène.

Roger Durieux, who preferred to be called Christian, came from Algeria and was the son of a low-ranking French civil servant. He had worked for some time for the French Secret

Meeting in Switzerland:
Bernt Engelmann on the left, talking to "little Napoléon" Christian
Durieux—a member of the French Secret Police, a cellar Casanova,
and an assassin. Note the swastika on his jacket.

Photo: Petra Engelmann, Hamburg

Service, DST, and since 1957 he was on "leave without pay,"
acting as liaison between Paris and the terrorists appointed to
eliminate the weapons merchants in Germany.

Anyone meeting the pale teen-ager would comment on his
striking resemblance to the young Napoléon Buonaparte, which
he emphasized by his prerehearsed Napoleonic gestures. Durieux
had disappeared on March 14, 1959, eleven days after Captain
Morris was killed in Frankfurt. On the night of the fourteenth,

in a Cologne nightclub, the trio—Durieux, Viari, and Pedro—celebrated until the next morning the successful completion of their assignment in Frankfurt and their temporary farewell from Germany. Then the trio vanished.

At the end of October, 1959, one member of the team reappeared on the scene: Christian Durieux.

This chapter began on a Sunday with a phone call I received from a friend, a Paris journalist, who knew about my interest in weapons dealers and their enemies.

"Are you interested in interviewing a leader of the Red Hand?" he asked. "He calls himself Christian Durieux."

What a question! Of course I wanted the interview.

But then my colleague added, "My intermediary is asking for a fee of only $10. He'll then bring you the assassins of Hamburg, Frankfurt, and Bonn—Durieux first."

With this my interest vanished.

"Someone is apparently trying to play a practical joke on us," I said. "Who would be willing to arrange an interview with men wanted by the police of three federal states for only $10?"

But I was wrong. Three weeks later the London *Daily Mail* published a cabled report by their Paris correspondent, Michael Jacobson. He had interviewed Christian Durieux.

As I was told later, Jacobson was at first extremely skeptical about this interview. He had paid a fee of $10. However, after the first few minutes of his meeting with Durieux, Jacobson's skepticism vanished. He realized to his astonishment that he had made a real catch. The man *was* Christian Durieux, a member of the Red Hand, and a participant in several spectacular assassination attempts.

On the following day, Jacobson wrote his report of the Durieux interview, and informed his editor of the sensational story. Two days later, on November 5, 1959, as agreed, Durieux returned to Jacobson to read the manuscript and authorize it for publication. Little Napoléon was accompanied by a bodyguard whom he called "Pedro," a man in his fifties with a boxer's face and a long, visible scar.

Before both men left, Jacobson asked: "What is your occupation? Should I mention it in the article? What is your place of birth and your present address?"

Durieux hesitated. Then he said: "You can say that I was born in Algeria, near Oran, but I am of Corsican descent. This is important. I live in Paris now, which is unimportant. I have four or five different addresses. And with regard to my occupation—you had better say civil servant."

Toward the end of November, the *Daily Mail* published the Durieux interview. It was copied by the world press, and caused a sensation, especially in Germany. It began with the following sentence: "I, Christian Durieux, am an active member of the Red Hand, a secret organization originally established in North Africa to take vengeance on the Arab Nationalists by using their own methods."

Concerning the attempted murders in Germany, little Napoléon was proud to have participated actively in the bombings of Otto Schlüter, Georg Puchert, and in the shooting of Dr. Ait Ahcène. "The Red Hand is proud of their actions, but not triumphant," ended his macabre report.

The interview earned the *Daily Mail* correspondent not only honors but all sorts of trouble. He was interrogated by the French security police, the Sûreté Nationale; they requested a photocopy of the original document bearing Durieux's signature, and concluded finally that Jacobson had interviewed an impostor. The Red Hand did not exist, nor did Christian Durieux. The French authorities had never issued an identity card for such a person. The whole affair was a hoax. When the culprit was caught, he would be confronted with Jacobson, and severely punished.

However, this confrontation never took place. The otherwise efficient French police were unable to locate little Napoléon in Paris or anywhere else.

Instead he turned up again in person. On December 5, 1959, at the Paris office of the German Press Agency (DPA, *Deutschen Presse Agentur*), appeared an unshaven, extremely nervous Durieux who swore he would tell the full truth this time.

He was hunted by the police, and in a hurry. Then he explained to the DPA's Paris chief, Hartmut Stein, that everything he had told Jacobson, the *Daily Mail* correspondent, was nonsense, a harmless hoax, nothing else!

Immediately after Durieux's departure from the DPA offices, the French Ministry of the Interior called Stein (on Saturday afternoon), and inquired whether Monsieur Durieux had visited him to deliver a retraction.

Stein was speechless.

Had not the Sûreté assured Jacobson that Durieux did not even exist?

And now this excess of official effort because of a hoax!

However, he forwarded Durieux's retraction to his editor in Germany.

Much later, Durieux told me what had induced him to take this step.

On December 2, 1959, shortly after publication of the *Daily Mail* interview, and three days before the DPA retraction, Chancellor Adenauer paid an official visit to President de Gaulle. The conference between the two statesmen proceeded amicably until the German Chancellor mentioned a delicate subject—the Red Hand.

De Gaulle's friendly expression turned to stone, and the Chancellor quickly changed the subject. Later, in his intimate circle, Adenauer admitted: "Monsieur de Gaulle considered this very improper."

However, the short intermezzo caused a big stir behind the scenes. The chief of the Sûreté Nationale was informed; the Minister of the Interior issued orders to suppress immediately every rumor about the Red Hand; the Counterintelligence Service received new directives; and the secret police summoned their inspector Christian Durieux, then on leave without pay.

Frightened out of his wits, little Napoléon approached a high-ranking friend and benefactor, lawyer Jean-Baptiste Biaggi, a representative for the Right Radical Party. He had actively participated in the overthrow of the Fourth Republic. And he was of Corsican descent. Biaggi had employed Durieux during the Fourth Republic to organize mass demonstrations and carry out terrorist acts to intimidate nervous members of parliament, thereby paving the way for seizure of power by De Gaulle.

However, Biaggi had switched sides and now supported the Right Wing opposition against De Gaulle, and was busily preparing another *coup d'état*. In his bedroom, serving also as a reception room for visitors, he kept a loaded gun on the nightstand. The young men in high boots and leather jackets who frequently visited his house were armed with guns and hand grenades.

The only unarmed confidant of Biaggi was a man who wore the habit of a Dominican monk, and who was his house chaplain and private secretary. Biaggi was just holding a meeting with him when Durieux visited. He advised his protégé to get in touch with the DST immediately and to prepare a retraction to quiet the Germans, using Biaggi as a reference. Then he patted Durieux's unshaven cheeks, gave him some money, and sent him on his way.

On December 6, 1959, Durieux's DPA retraction appeared in all German newspapers: The story published by the *Daily Mail* should be considered a hoax and pure nonsense. He was surprised that the Germans had believed such a fairy tale.

The audacity of little Napoléon to play his little jokes with the world press increased my desire to meet him. I decided to start inquiries immediately and find out all I could about him before scheduling a personal meeting. Again, luck was with me.

A few days after the second Durieux interview had been published, while buying cigarettes at a small tobacco shop in Mönckebergstrasse in Hamburg, I met a colleague. We discussed the Durieux case, and I noticed that the young salesclerk listened very attentively to our conversation. After my colleague left, I asked the interested young man whether he knew the person we had talked about.

He said hesitantly that he was not quite sure. Did I have a

photograph of the man? I did not, but I knew that the Frankfurt police had one in their files because shortly after Heinz Wolf had issued arrest warrants for the three Red Hands, he received an anonymous letter containing a snapshot of Durieux among a group of young people in a beer garden. One person was marked with a cross: little Napoléon.

With some persuasion I obtained a copy, had Christian Durieux's head enlarged, and went again to the tobacco shop on Mönckebergstrasse.

"Yes, that's the man," said the salesclerk after looking at the photograph. "He looked just like that then."

"Then" was the winter of 1954. The young man and a girl he intended to marry took a French-language course at the Institute for Languages. The young French teacher, Monsieur Durieux, had been the cause of breaking up their engagement.

I was given some helpful information I could use as a basis for continuing my inquiries, and after several visits, starting with the office of the Institute for Languages, many taverns and restaurants, landladies, and the correspondent for a Swedish newspaper, I not only knew Durieux's life story but also some piquant details.

It was sheer coincidence that I discovered a school friend of little Napoléon, a young French-Algerian dentist who had just opened his practice in Switzerland and who had no active interest in politics.

I was enthusiastic enough to travel to Switzerland, and to get to talk with him, I had a filling put in one of my teeth.

This is the story of the assassin Christian Durieux, compiled from many small details:

He was the son of a police officer, and grew up in Algeria, in a small provincial town. During his youth he had witnessed the treatment of the native Algerians as inferiors, and had seen his father beat up Algerian prisoners as soon as they were brought before him. Not even the strongest Arab boy would dare to defend himself when attacked by young Durieux, who was a small, weak boy.

In Oran, where he went to high school with Algerian girls,

he took every advantage of his privileges as a white boy and the son of a gendarme. He developed into a positive social menace.

One night, he entered the dormitory of a girls' school through the window, but experienced his first defeat: The alert Sisters of the Holy Heart discovered him in a student's bed, and gave him such a sound beating with leather straps and broomsticks that he fled in terror, limping and screaming, and had to seek medical treatment for his wounds.

When he failed his final exams, his father sent him to France. There he finished his education at a boarding school.

His military service was in Germany—in the Pfalz garrison of a French artillery regiment. From there he was sent to a cadet training school in Idar-Oberstein, but joined the police force instead—the Secret Police, DST. He was assigned as an interpreter for West Algerian and Moroccan dialects to a special brigade whose task was to keep close surveillance on the growing nationalist tendencies among the North Africans.

During the summer of 1954, shortly before the outbreak of the Algerian war, Inspector Durieux was granted leave of absence, and traveled, via Germany, to Denmark and Sweden. He joined a group of French actors, who arranged little theater evenings in Swedish castles and country towns.

Wherever Christian Durieux and his friends appeared, there were minor scandals. The people who had very justifiable complaints about the troupe's wild habits were mostly the fathers of pretty daughters or the elderly husbands of beautiful women; sometimes even the ladies themselves had unpleasant experiences with members of the group when they missed their jewels or large amounts of cash. This lasted for one long Swedish summer. Then the troupe, and Durieux with them, transferred their activities to the Swedish capital. The lively actors remained in Stockholm until the spring of 1957, and their departure coincided with the forcible dissolution by the Stockholm Vice Squad of a rather interesting circle.

This circle was called the "Bango Club," and had exhausted the patience of the Stockholm law-enforcement authorities not only because precocious high-school girls—and effeminate boys—were introduced there to society ladies and elderly gentlemen but also because a number of blackmail cases resulted from these meetings. And there were other embarrassing incidents: the appearance of a diplomat's fifteen-year-old daughter among the Bango Club's debutantes, and the disappearance of highly confidential documents from her father's embassy office.

The Swedish police broke up the convivial circle, and requested the club to depart immediately from Sweden's shores for good.

It should be mentioned here that the name of the club secretary was Christian Durieux and that he left Stockholm for Hamburg, where he had lived previously for several months in 1954–1955.

Christian Durieux's Hamburg performances were somewhat similar to those in Sweden, only the environment was less refined.

Most of the time he prowled around disreputable cellar bars, and when he ran out of money, he provided companionship for well-off middle-aged women or tried his luck as a quick-sketch and quick-change artist in third-class nightclubs. In Hamburg he soon got into trouble with the Vice Squad, though not because he may have befriended some widow. His trouble came as assistant French teacher in the Language Institute.

There Durieux had not only seduced the prospective fiancée of my cigarette salesman but also many other, much younger, students. These teen-agers were so enthusiastic about the fiery little Corsican that they were readily available for passionate hours of love, in single order; they also were at his disposal for pornographic group scenes. The genuinely versatile French teacher photographed these scenes with the aid of an automatic shutter release, enlarged the snapshots to postcard size, and in order to raise his living standard, had them sold by some of his friends at the Reeperbahn, Hamburg's amusement center.

His activities were discovered when an uncle from the provinces bought a card during a tour of St. Pauli's attractions to produce at his regular outing with his friends in his hometown tavern, and to his distress recognized his little niece among these licentious teen-agers.

Durieux's life story could be continued indefinitely, but between the many coarse, erotic, and evil activities of this young man who found work so repulsive are several points that deserve more attention than his varied but repetitious debaucheries.

There were unmistakable signs that Durieux, during his stay in Germany, had busied himself not only with sex but with other bombs as well. His sojourns in Hamburg, Bonn, and Frankfurt coincided in each case with both attempted and successful assassinations, and he had been seen in the company of Jean Viari and Pedro.

All this and the statements and retractions of Durieux in November, 1959, had aroused my curiosity, so I decided to make every effort to meet the young man.

However, it would take several weeks and a great deal of patience before a meeting could be arranged. Again the contact man was a French journalist, one who did not conceal his sympathy with the Red Hand. He also laid down conditions for the meeting: absolute discretion; the meeting was to take place in neutral territory; all expenses were to be paid by my employer, including a bodyguard for little Napoléon; and, finally, one condition that made the journalistic character of the meeting questionable: Through my assistance, Durieux was willing to make his peace with the German authorities and the Algerian FLN, whose vengeance he had begun to fear.

We finally agreed that I was to inform Wolf of the planned meeting and to secure safe-conduct for Durieux to a border railroad station where he could meet with Wolf's interrogation officers; however, this would take place *after* the interview.

Regarding the presence of an FLN representative, I had contacted Ait Ahcène's successor, the Algerian Ambassador in

Bonn, Hafid Keramane, who was then at the head of the Red Hand blacklist. He and his assistant would participate in the meeting and help to "bring the truth to light." This, he said, he owed the Red Hand's victims.

All participants would be unarmed.

I called my contact, setting out the conditions. An hour later he returned the call and said that Durieux had accepted. He was willing to give his word of honor to be unarmed. (It turned out that this agreement was strictly adhered to by all but one—Durieux himself.)

The evening before the rendezvous—a Saturday—I met my French colleague in the waiting room at the Lausanne railroad station. We had agreed on a late hour for a preliminary conference, and expected the place to be empty.

However, we discovered quite a few gentlemen intently studying the latest issues of the daily paper, watching our every move.

And then our eyes popped: The waiting room looked like the assembly of an international police congress!

I recognized not less than three officers of the German Federal Criminal Police plus a gentleman from the Frankfurt Homicide Squad who was assigned to the Puchert case. My contact in an instant recognized four representatives of the Lyon DST branch, and of the others, one did not need much imagination. They would be the Swiss counterparts of the Germans and the French.

Now what should we do?

Since my intended interview with Durieux had apparently developed into a public affair, should we abandon our hard-earned meeting? Or could we fool the secret police from three countries? We decided on the latter, but I do not intend to disclose how it was done. We succeeded, but describing how we eluded them might jeopardize my newly restored harmony with the police.

That next morning, well rested and refreshed, I had breakfast with Durieux at a place forty-five miles from Lausanne, but

I was irked that I had to wear light-brown sandals with a double-breasted, dark-blue suit. (My black shoes remained at the door of my hotel room in Lausanne together with two unobtrusive-looking gentlemen who at this early hour of the morning were still calm and composed.)

Also disconcerting, but of no personal concern to me, was Durieux's appearance: The breast pocket of his blazer was adorned with the insignia of the Hitler party—an eagle, carrying in its talons an oakleaf wreath and a swastika.

To wear this outfit in Switzerland in 1960 was an outrage. But Durieux's behavior was illogical. Durieux and the French journalist acting as contact man began to praise the Führer and the SS, just as some weapons dealers did—Ernst Wilhelm Springer, for example. And when they assured me that their battle against the Semitic Algerians was only a continuation of the "battle of the Western world against the common enemy, Judaism," I recalled the comments of Krüger, the lawyer–weapons dealer, and author of the book *The Jews in England*. Other parallels could be drawn between the weapons merchants and their Red Hand persecutors. Their uninhibited consumption of food and drink paid for by someone else reminded me of Seidenschnur (the difference being his elegance and refined taste); and little Napoléon's bragging about sex recalled old J. J. Petersen's.

Forgetting these side issues, the meeting for which we had expended so much effort and money proved unproductive. I could fill some gaps in Christian Durieux's biography, but he could not provide any substantially new material. Regarding his participation in the bombings, he was very uncooperative; his statements were vague and generalized.

"I support my statement to the press!" he said with fervor, and brushed a Napoléonic lock from his forehead.

"Which one do you mean?" I asked politely. "The first or the second statement?"

"The first one, of course!" replied Durieux. "The report in the *Daily Mail,* which I approved, is true. I was forced to the retraction by unforeseen circumstances."

"If I remember the *Daily Mail* statement correctly, you are proud of the Puchert and Ait Ahcène murders, the slayings of Schlüter's mother and his business partner?" I continued.

Durieux did not hesitate: "Yes, of course, but we are not triumphant."

These were the same words he had used in the Paris interview with Michael Jacobson, and he added: "I don't want to say any more on this subject. After all, we are speaking about murders, you understand?"

I understood, and said quickly: "If you do not want to discuss the murders that have been committed, perhaps you would like to talk about the attempted murders. How can you explain that one or another in a group has been spared?"

Durieux smiled. "We know them all," he said, and frowned just as the young Napoléon might have done. "If people like Seidenschnur or Krüger in Hamburg have been spared so far, there are special reasons!"

He fell silent, and as much as I tried, he would not talk any more.

Despite these meager results, I was quite satisfied with the interview. Admittedly, I had not gained any new information, but a personal impression was more revealing than a thousand files. This unscrupulous little adventurer and muddlehead sitting in front of me was the explanation of many puzzling aspects. What I had already suspected was true: The weapons merchants and their enemies were birds of a feather. Their environment, their interests, even their jargon, were the same.

"Why," I inquired before we parted, "are the weapons merchants persecuted by the Red Hand?"

"Partly for political reasons," replied little Napoléon without hesitation, "because they support our enemies. But that is not all. The motives are mainly to be found in morals, because dealing in weapons is the dirtiest business imaginable!"

With this I let the matter rest, but I could well imagine some work that seemed several degrees dirtier, remembering his sordid life story. I did not need to delve into the past; the future would provide a surprise that could not be more ironic.

Because of his blatant bragging, Durieux as a secret agent

was no longer useful. The French government was working on a peaceful settlement with Algeria, and was to give up this persistently defeated last bastion in Africa. The terrorists now had to seek new employment. Durieux transferred his activities to a new area of unrest: the Belgian Congo.

He was employed in Katanga as a secret police officer for the black dictator Tshombé. And then, when the battles became fiercer, he took part in the "dirtiest business imaginable"—weapons dealings.

Together with the previously mentioned contact man, he supplied arms to the black Katanga insurgents for their battle against the UN troops.

I was never to encounter the two again, and had no desire to meet any other Red Hand members. But one incident must be reported:

After our meeting, Durieux took the shortest route to Basle, where, in a quiet office in the railroad station, the meeting between little Napoléon and Wolf's officers took place. The conference was brief and without the desired result, because even though Durieux offered to reveal the identities of his accomplices and supporters, his request for safe-conduct and asylum in West Germany could not be granted.

An hour later little Napoléon left hurriedly for France. In his nervous haste he forgot his luggage, a black briefcase whose contents appropriately symbolized the Red Hand. To their amazement, the police found a pair of pajamas, a comb and a toothbrush, a large-caliber gun loaded with six bullets, a king-size bottle of sweet-smelling jasmine perfume, and two dozen picture postcards of the type Durieux had distributed in Hamburg.

Cheap perfume, dirty postcards, and a gun—pledged by Durieux's word of honor he would not carry. These were all that remained in Germany of the Red Hand, not counting the dead and injured.

BUBI'S BICYCLES

MANY BITTER DISAPPOINTMENTS, like the useless weapons from Czechoslovakia sold by Krüger and Springer, caused the Algerians to be extremely careful. Several weeks after that fiasco, another former SS officer appeared in Rabat offering his services as a weapons merchant. He claimed to be a proved friend of the Arab people. This weapons merchant was a somewhat different type; he was not a citizen of the West German Federal Republic, but Austrian, residing in Vienna. He referred to himself as a merchant, indicating by this designation more optimism and faith in the future than sense of reality.

His name was Franz Wimmer, but he preferred to call himself Wimmer-Lanquet, and if circumstances should warrant it, Franz von Wimmer-Lanquet.

During World War II, Intelligence Officer Wimmer had been assigned temporarily to the Arab Legion and had obtained the rank of SS *Obersturmbannführer,* which motivated him to introduce himself in Rabat as "Colonel von Wimmer." He informed the Moroccan authorities that he represented a large international armaments organization consisting of German-Austrian and Swiss firms founded by a leading industrialist, Baron Peter Alexander von le Fort.

The Moroccans showed mixed emotions. Some were partly impressed and some only polite, determined not to be cheated again. Those with strong determinations were mostly men, but the majority of the genuinely impressed group were young women, educated in Europe and now leading members of Moroccan high society. However, their interest was not so much concentrated on Wimmer's organization and its weapons offers as on the strapping blond colonel himself, with whom they had tea on shady verandas or in cool salons, protected from the burning sun by tightly draped curtains, whenever there was an opportunity.

It was not long before Colonel von Wimmer was the cock of the roost in Rabat high society. Soon he had his first business discussions, and the other leading figures in his firm were revealed.

The head man was—and here Wimmer did not exaggerate —Hitler's commissioner for the Olympic Games, Baron von le Fort. He was the real creator of the organization behind Wimmer, but was interested only in the overall planning and the expected profits. The actual work had to be done by others. He was very favorably impressed with one gentleman, a dashing, man-of-the-world type whose father had been Paymaster General in the Prussian Army.

This was Seidenschnur from the Bonn Liaison Office of Belgian Armaments Manufacturers who at the time had the valuable support and assistance of a rather gullible person—a former high-ranking civil servant, Dr. Erwin Muermann. Dr. Muermann, towed along by the agile Seidenschnur, not only provided the Bonn Liaison Office with the distinction of high officialdom but also paid all expenses willingly.

Fortified and encouraged by Baron von le Fort, Seidenschnur had written a memorandum that described the situation as follows:

The Belgian arms industry, assisted by the United States and investments by major organizations who made large

profits in the former colonies, has expanded considerably.
It is a well-known fact that the old established reputable
arms and ammunition works in the Liège area are ex-
periencing marketing difficulties. Because of their financial
association with major companies in France, even the most
potentially promising Belgian manufacturers are unable to
supply profitable markets directly, for instance the Algerian
Liberation Army. The small manufacturers are still further
discouraged from taking part in the potential African business for fear of political consequences. Here is where our
organization steps in, and we offer our services (against a
fee covering our expenses and including an appropriate
commission) as agents for "triangular" business deals.

In fact, the Bonn Liaison Office represented about a dozen
Belgian firms anxious to export their products (and willing to
pay expenses), including the Poudreries Réunies de Zeebrugge
(United Gunpowder Works) and gun factories in the Liège
area. The Bonn Liaison Office connected with Baron von le Fort
would open the North African market for the products of the
Belgian arms manufacturers—through a firm with the bizarre
name of NAWILAND. (All this happened long before Puchert's
appearance in Germany.)
    NAWILAND was not, as could be assumed, located in the
heart of Africa, but constituted the Alpine wing of a new
weapons syndicate with its head office in Vaduz, the rural-look-
ing capital of the Principality of Liechtenstein. NAWILAND
was represented by a mailbox and a sign that read:

NAWILAND TRUST Reg., Vaduz
Import—Export—Transit Agency

This firm was established with one main objective—to
evade income tax. It consisted of three partners, two of whom
had invested little more than the first syllable of their names: Dr.
Heinrich NAtlacen, forty-nine, owner of an abrasive and polish-

ing material shop in Stanislausgasse in Vienna; and "Colonel," retired, Franz WImmer, forty-five. The third member of the team was the Swiss liqueur manufacturer Werner LANDtwing, fifty-eight, the senior partner, who was the only actual financier of the new enterprise. He had acquired wealth through the manufacture of pure cherry brandy and other spirits—wealth he intended to increase by his partnership in the promising weapons business.

According to strict Liechtenstein law, every organization residing in this good country must include a local citizen, and therefore the team was joined by Privy Councilor Dr. Ritter, financial adviser to the ruling prince.

The commercial success of NAWILAND and also the Bonn Liaison Office of Belgian Armaments Manufacturers had thus far been limited, the principal activities consisting of the accumulation of expenses. Now a really big deal would net some large profits, and it was initiated by a coordination of common interests and the dispatch of Colonel Wimmer to Morocco.

To facilitate communications between Vienna, Lausanne, Bonn, and Rabat, a special code was established. Code words and camouflage names were invented to cover their true identities and purposes, and as a protection against curious people. Colonel Wimmer's pseudonym was "Bubi"; for special assignments it was "Victoria." Financier Landtwing was rechristened "Lindwurm"; and Dr. Erwin Muermann, the retired civil servant now employed as a courier, appeared as "Mümmelmann" in the business correspondence. "One crate of lemons" stood for 1,000 rounds of ammunition, whereby the requested caliber fell freely and easily into place, according to the item appearing on the order with the lemon crates. For example, if an order was for "approximately 10,000 bicycles, 5 crates lemons," 10,000 98K carbines with 5,000 rounds of ammunition, caliber 7.92 were requested. If the order was for "plows," it meant machine guns of the MG42 type.

Strange telegrams were exchanged between Rabat, Vienna, and Bonn. It soon became apparent that Bubi's demands were more than the stocks the Belgians behind Mümmelmann and Seidenraupe (Seidenschnur) had available.

However, other arms manufacturers could be found in Europe. The organization's catalog became thicker and thicker. For instance, a special attraction was "portable radios." This pseudonym concealed, according to the code book, "explosives charges, 1½ meters long, which can be screwed together or laid out side by side. They are very suitable against barbed wire barriers. Ignition can be effected electrically or by hand grenades."

Another novelty was mines with twenty-minute delayed fuses (code name, "tape recorder parts"). "As you know," Bubi wrote to Seidenraupe, "the whole of Algeria is surrounded by an electric barbed-wire fence. If it is cut, machine-gun fire is directed automatically to this point, and there are always many casualties. The time-fuse mines are required to remove these obstacles and at the same time escape the enemy fire."

Seidenraupe and Mümmelmann started a search for half a million mines. The appropriate time fuses were to be procured from a Nuremberg watch factory.

All partners were of untiring diligence, and did their best to fill all orders and obtain everything requested by Wimmer-Bubi. One of his letters read: "In the near future I expect a firm order of such gigantic proportions that our organization should receive the Finance Ministry's highest commendation. This order should be the biggest ever received by a private organization."

Seidenraupe wrote to his bank, which despite its willingness to participate, still retained a healthy measure of mistrust: "Our man in Morocco enjoys the special benevolence of a Moroccan royal princess. Consequently, we can count on the support of the royal court, a fact that will, of course, help to remove otherwise insurmountable obstacles and be of favorable influence to our cause. Also, a male member of the Sultan's family is an inactive partner of our Moroccan enterprise."

These indiscreet hints, like all of Seidenraupe's statements, contained a grain of truth. But neither the fancies of a princess nor the inactive demands of a prince could, in the long run, seriously influence the course of events.

For some time everything went according to plan.

When Lindwurm-Landtwing voiced some doubts about reimbursement for his high advance payments plus the accrued interest, Seidenraupe consoled him with a letter, which said in part:

> The heavy and lighter merchandise reserved for our organization represents a material reserve of at least $7,500,-000. To this amount should be added the value of the merchandise that is available for our disposal in the Belgian works and also in Turkey; not to mention the smaller lots from other countries.

In fact, there was hardly an arms factory between Tampere and Istanbul, Zeebrugge and Pilsen that had not been tapped by the indefatigable Seidenraupe. And how eager all large and small firms were to take part in the North African weapons business!

Brussels' Eau, Gaz, Electricité et Applications, a big syndicate working with Belgian French capital investments, hurriedly replied to Wimmer-Bubi's high-explosive tape recorder request: "Please let us know whether the Moroccan firm has already obtained an import license. We are particularly interested in remaining the sole supplier in this business deal."

Seidenraupe was received by General Director Caesar of the Düsseldorf Rheinmetall works, who considered production of MG42 machine guns for Wimmer-Bubi-Victoria's customers.

And Mümmelmann was plainly besieged by the Deutsche Flugdienst GmbH in Frankfurt, a subsidiary of Lufthansa and the German Federal Railways, that wanted permission for the establishment of an arms airlift between Vienna and Casablanca.

The Belgian armaments expert, Albert Peltier, owner of the arms factory La Précision Liègeoise in Herbesthal near

Liège, was working on a proposal for the construction of modern arms and ammunition factories on the Moroccan-Algerian border. Bubi commented on this: "98K carbines, NATO assault guns, automatic pistols, and machine guns of the 34 and 42 types will be manufactured there. Supervisors to train a local work force are required."

Seidenraupe and his friends expected to act as agents in this project—for a high fee, of course, and maybe a partnership. But the project failed.

However, the syndicate soon completed a successful transaction. After prolonged bartering, Mümmelmann—dispatched to Rabat for the purpose of reinforcing Bubi—obtained a substantial order: infantry ammunition amounting to about $350,-000.

Before they could secure the order, the organization had to overcome an obstacle that had seriously threatened the transaction: a competitive bid by the Basle weapons dealer Max Zimmerli, considered more favorable by the Moroccans.

Seidenraupe, at his home base, alarmed by Mümmelmann and pressed hard by Lindwurm, decided on a radical method to avoid further expenses.

He had heard that the troublesome Zimmerli was in the hospital awaiting amputation of his leg. Seidenraupe cabled to Rabat: "Zimmerli's bids have no substantial backing because he died in the hospital. His backers are not known. Peace be with him. Kind regards, Seidenraupe."

The death announcement finally defeated their competitor. Mümmelmann proudly presented the order for infantry ammunition.

The elation over this success did not last long because the organization found the Moroccan order extremely difficult to fill. Though the Moroccans requested outdated calibers of 11.8 or 7.3 millimeters that were nearly impossible to find, they were located finally—in some small factories in France.

Seidenraupe's tireless creative efforts obtained the seemingly impossible. In several weeks the whole unusual assortment of outdated ammunition was brought together, and, assisted by

Weapons sales negotiation in pajamas:
Swiss competitor Zimmerli (seated)—declared dead by "Seidenraupe"
(in background).

Photo: Collection Bernt Engelmann

a surreptitiously obtained export license, was shipped from France to Hamburg.

But then troublesome NATO restrictions had to be eluded. Seidenraupe had already chartered a Scandinavian ship, and was just having the merchandise loaded—declared as official Moroccan export—when the country was declared a "troubled area" and, according to a NATO agreement, shipments of war matériel were prohibited. Bonn refused the export permit.

It took weeks before Seidenraupe found a way out. "I rearranged the entire transaction," he explained to me later. And so it was accomplished: While the ammunition was stored in Hamburg, incurring interest and demurrage charges, Seidenraupe searched for and found a man who, for $12,500, provided a forged Certificate of Use. The certificate provided him with the export license. With Alexandria as the alleged destination, a Swedish freighter carried the prized merchandise to the real destination—Tangier.

For their anxiety and trouble, the organization made a clear profit of roughly $75,000. Because of the difficult procurement, the wholesale price had risen to $232,000. Transportation, insurance, interest on loans, demurrage, and other charges had cost approximately $29,000, with $12,500 added for the forged document. The actual retail price was $348,400.

The profits, of course, were to be divided: $37,500 for the NAWILAND partners, $37,500 for the Bonn Liaison Office—that is, Messrs. Mümmelmann and Seidenraupe—and a small percentage out of the total for Baron von le Fort, who had been the matchmaker for the groups.

But, typical of the weapons business, some were left out or put off; others got their share and paid their most pressing debts; and one person—Seidenraupe—received a double share, without a thought of his obligations to others, especially the useful Mümmelmann. Seidenraupe's creditors were put off with the good news cabled to him by Wimmer-Bubi from Rabat—another, much more substantial order could be expected!

Colonel Wimmer actually did obtain a second, much larger

order for antitank weapons, bazookas, mines, and tape-recorder parts, amounting to about $1,500,000.

The payment, according to Paragraph 2 in the contract negotiated and signed in Tangier, would be made in cash after delivery and inspection by the buyer. The money would be deposited with and kept in trust by the governor of Tangier, Dr. Ben Jelloun. This was an unusual arrangement, but it was a precautionary measure insisted upon by the Moroccans, who wanted the transaction kept absolutely secret.

The suppliers also were taking no chances. NAWILAND obtained a Certificate of Use from the Swiss, stating that the war matériel was for the use of the British Army in Cyprus. A certificate based on such a claim was the best possible guaranty to ensure safe passage through the French blockade. The document cost $150,000, 10 percent of the retail price, and was divided by the agents: a Swiss engineer from Zofingen and his Paris contact—a NATO administrator.

Now the Danish freighter *Bornholm* (2,800 tons) could sail without fear of French controls, with its hold bulging with crates of Czech weapons, eagerly awaited in North Africa.

The ability of this bizarre team to procure antitank weapons from behind the Iron Curtain and to dispatch them to North Africa with so little effort was due to the excellent contacts of Dr. Natlacen.

His life was interesting and adventurous. He had fought against Franco in the International Brigade, and in World War II he led Indian freedom fighters against their colonial oppressors. He joined an Indian sect, and mastered Yoga. He not only used it to strengthen his body and his spiritual powers but also to facilitate his business transactions. He was known to have "extraordinary faculties"—according to a sober report that financier Landtwing obtained on his new NAWILAND partner through an information bureau. In practice, Dr. Natlacen used his Yoga training by going into a deep trance just prior to a difficult business transaction; and his beautiful secretary and confidante, Anita, wrote down every word that escaped his lips during this stage of absolute concentration.

He then faithfully followed his abstracted advice, allegedly with surprising results.

However, there was another, more earthly way Dr. Natlacen obtained useful information and insight. This way led through the Iron Curtain, right to Prague, to the offices of the arms and ammunition department of the government-owned Czech trading agency Omnipol.

One step along the way was an attaché of the Czechoslovakian Embassy in Vienna, in whose breast pocket Dr. Natlacen's letters to Prague traveled every weekend. The replies by the Omnipol officials were transmitted every Monday morning to Stanislausgasse where Dr. Natlacen and the beautiful Anita had taken up residence.

In a safe behind a cabinet containing his abrasive and polishing materials, Dr. Natlacen deposited the Czech weapons bids that constituted the basis for the Liechtenstein organization's transactions with the Moroccans, conceived in Yoga trance.

There were orders for machine guns of the 42-type copied from the German model, with a replacement barrel for a price of $310 (Rheinmetall in Düsseldorf asked a minimum price of $500); brand-new army carbines 98K with brand-new ammunition; copied bazookas; also Tatra trucks, $13,000 cheaper than comparable models from the West. Everything far below market prices.

The organization's future seemed rosy. Landtwing in Schwyz and Seidenraupe in Bonn visualized themselves swimming in money. Wimmer-Bubi in Rabat was a little more skeptical. He was the one who stood in the front line of battle where it was not too hard to see that there was a certain reluctance on the part of the Moroccans.

Then it happened that one of Wimmer's Moroccan ladies informed her dear blond colonel, during a tête-à-tête, that her husband, with whom she was not at all in love because her marriage was a social arrangement only, had given her a tip: the charming German agent would be fired.

Morocco, her husband had explained, was short of cash,

Swastika trademark:
factory-fresh carbines made in Czechoslovakia's
Skoda Works, with faked Third Reich trademarks.

Photos: Collection Bernt Engelmann

and, by Allah! this was true, at least where government finances were concerned. But, on the other hand, Morocco was rich in citrus fruit, phosphate, and other treasures of nature. And his own family, in particular, had an abundance of oranges, lemons, and other fruit. However, the demand for war matériel was so enormous, especially since their Algerian allies were still fighting for their freedom, that a better solution had to be found than paying for arms with hard dollars. What Morocco, and especially her dear husband, had in mind was a gigantic exchange deal—weapons for oranges!

Perhaps the good broad-shouldered friend could talk his associates into giving their consent to such an exchange. The colonel could convey to his partners the advantages of such a business in two directions: They would profit on the oranges as well as on the weapons.

Wimmer inquired about the destination of the fruit.

"Well, maybe Czechoslovakia," said the lady. Wimmer was alerted.

Now he understood what the Moroccans planned: They wanted to use his organization to establish their own contacts with the Czechs, and they would then deal directly, eliminating NAWILAND and Seidenraupe and his partner Mümmelmann.

A realistic but very disconcerting plan, he thought, but why did the queen of his heart tell him about it?

He looked at her, and despite the fact that she was a society lady directly related to the ruling royal dynasty, she winked at him and said: "It will not be to your disadvantage, *chéri*. How would you like a 5 percent interest in our citrus export, with a proper contract, of course, and payments to a bank account in Switzerland?"

Wimmer asked for some time to consider the proposal, dispatched a cable to the Yoga doctor in Vienna and to the busy Seidenraupe in Bonn, and called the organization together. They met in Switzerland, and after a long discussion Wimmer-Bubi persuaded his friends to introduce the Moroccans to the Czechs so that the million-dollar deals might increase to multimillion-dollar deals.

Greed was triumphant over common sense. The organization agreed, and the colonel cabled to Rabat: "Agree on 7 instead of 5 percent. Arrangement as requested immediately effective."

Late that night the reply arrived. It was brief, but Colonel Wimmer was satisfied: "Agree with 6 plus, my dear," it read.

The next morning, before he returned to Rabat, Wimmer met his partners at the breakfast table. They were wildly enthusiastic about selling oranges and lemons acquired with weapons.

They completely overlooked the fact that their lucrative triangular business would soon develop into a noncash, bilateral agreement. The branch on which they sat, waiting like vultures, they cut off themselves.

Three weeks later, in the spring of 1958, shortly before Puchert's journey to Germany, a group of gentlemen met in Lausanne, in the Château d'Ouchy: two Czech diplomats; the Moroccan representative Si Abdelkébir, and two agents, Dr. Natlacen and Seidenschnur.

Wimmer had cabled his congratulations from Rabat, and his regrets that he was needed elsewhere and therefore unable to participate. Actually, he was not particularly interested in the outcome of the Lausanne conference.

After two days of negotiations, an exchange agreement on the "orange business" was drafted. But Seidenschnur steered immediately for a final contract, specifying the fees for the entire organization and especially for himself. But the Czechs and Moroccans refused. They had no authority to sign contracts.

And the disaster took its course.

Soon after these informal discussions, an official trade mission traveled from Czechoslovakia to Rabat, and then a Moroccan minister—a close relative of the husband of Wimmer's lady —flew to Prague.

An exchange agreement in the amount of about $10,000,-000 secured Czech weapons for Morocco in exchange for oranges and lemons supplied by a company that enjoyed the support of the Moroccan government.

The partners, completely bypassed, quarreled at length over the high expenses, particularly three items—Wimmer's daily flower arrangement for a certain lady, his expensive room at the Hotel Tour Hassan, and extensive beverage consumption.

In the end, Mümmelmann and the wealthy liqueur manufacturer from Schwyz paid the bill.

Then everyone went on his way—Seidenschnur directly to Georg Puchert, who had just arrived from Tangier.

Dr. Natlacen resignedly wrote to Seidenschnur: "We have made a mistake somewhere. The 'orange business' alone would have been enough to keep us in money and away from work forever."

Seidenschnur replied: "People like Springer and Krüger make the mistakes, and we take the punishment for them."

The Moroccan special representative, Si Abdelkébir, whom I met later, said simply: "You know, if two governments do their own business, there is not too much cheating."

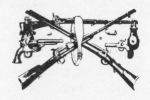

THE RED
NOTEBOOK

AFTER MY TRYING INVESTIGATION of the motives behind Puchert's assassination and the attempted murders of other weapons dealers, their friends, and employers, I felt I deserved a vacation. I had interviewed many people involved or concerned with the bombings, and had gained not only professional recognition but also the reputation as an expert on the weapons merchants and their trade, extending from mid-Europe to North Africa.

I needed to get away from it all and to forget my Accounting Department, who were still showing the deepest displeasure about my expense accounts, which they approved only with the greatest reluctance.

I set out on an automobile trip, without plan or destination. Avoiding the main highways, I traveled through the picturesque hamlets and towns of southwest Germany. Wherever I found a comfortable inn, I stayed, until my desire to see the mountains urged me to continue my southward journey. When news was broadcast I switched my car radio off or turned the dial to another station. Even at the breakfast table I resisted the temptation to read the world news in the local papers, and after one week I could walk past a newsstand without giving it a second glance.

After two, three weeks—I had lost all count of time—I finally found, in southern Switzerland, a small hotel offering a magnificent view of the mountains and a lake; and with a sun balcony and comfortable armchairs, it left nothing to be desired.

I checked in and enjoyed the leisure of watching the activities of about a dozen fellow vacationers. There were two middle-aged married couples from provincial German towns who quickly made friends with each other and went on small trips together, the pleasures of which they discussed in the evenings over native red wine. The husbands were constantly on the lookout for a third man whom they could induce to take part in a proposed card game, in the meantime playing another, only moderately exciting game. The wives discussed in detail the professional and married lives of their grown children, and critically observed the other guests.

Then there were two Dutch women, around thirty, wearing unattractive but comfortable-looking walking shoes, and enjoying hearty appetites; an amply adorned widow from Luxembourg, constantly reading a voluminous French novel; a fragile lady of undeterminable age from Wiesbaden, looking for someone to listen to a detailed report on her many, very complicated operations. And there was the bikini girl.

She was a stunning blonde, who appeared only on rare occasions, always wearing a provocative, very brief white bikini, contrasting pleasantly with her suntanned skin, threatening, in a rather breathtaking manner, to slip off at the very next movement.

Of course, the bikini girl was not alone, and her existing or nonexisting marriage certificate constituted an endless conversation piece for the other ladies.

The man was a young Italian, perhaps two or three years younger, about twenty-three. Except for his low forehead, he was good looking, tall, and strongly built, with gleaming white teeth and chestnut-colored, closely cropped hair.

And also vacationing at the hotel were a lively man from Stuttgart and his thirteen-year-old son, Klaus. The wife was left behind to supervise the family's move to a new house. Klaus told this story to everybody in the hotel, and his father, a successful insurance agent, supplemented it by all sorts of little jokes. He also had something to say to everybody: clumsy compliments to the elderly ladies, more or less harmless jokes for the gentlemen, and an appreciative whistle when the bikini girl swung her hips as if they had built-in ball bearings. However, I enjoyed being with this small group, and I would have remained there, relaxingly bored, until the end of my vacation had it not been for Klaus, who found an object which he showed to everybody, hopefully waiting to be rewarded with some ice cream by the owner.

"I found it at the door of the phone booth," said Klaus, who looked at me expectantly. "Is this your book?" I gave an evasive answer, praised his untiring attention, and accepted it.

It was a small notebook bound in red leather, devoid of entries, apart from two phone numbers scribbled on the last page. The notebook was apparently an advertising promotion given to friends and customers by a large organization whose name appeared in prominent gold-embossed letters on the front page: INTERNATIONAL ARMAMENT CORPORATION. The front page was adorned with a coat of arms, but the delicate engraving did not fit the martial object too well—it displayed old-fashioned war equipment with regimental flags swelled out over crossed cannons, rifles, pistols, and battle-axes; cannon balls were cleanly stacked together, and the entire symbol was framed by a banderole with the inscription, in Latin, ESSE QUAM VIDERI, a free translation of which would be "To be rather than to seem."

I had not heard of this corporation. What was behind its pretentious trademark?

The next page contained the following advertisement:

International Armament Corporation
Import-Export Agency
Weapons, Ammunition, and Equipment
Main Offices in Washington, D.C.,
London, and Geneva
Office of the President and European Headquarters:
Salzburg, Austria, Rainerstrasse 26

And to emphasize their worldwide distribution, all the branch offices from about three dozen countries were listed in small type, from Panama to Switzerland, from Canada to Rhodesia.

I thought about it, and returned the book to Klaus.

"No," I said, "it does not belong to me. But I would be glad if you could let me know who the owner is. This is going to be a very interesting case, and like real detectives we might solve it together, and in between we could keep up our strength with ice cream."

Klaus seemed to accept this idea enthusiastically, but he then had doubts whether he would ever be able to find the owner. "I've asked just about all the guests," he said sadly. In a flash I suddenly knew who the owner of the red notebook was.

"Did you ask the biki—I mean the blonde lady in the pretty white swimsuit?" I asked my new partner. "I don't know her name, but I think she lives in Room 11."

"With her friend, the Italiano," finished Klaus, grinning happily. "She drives a red Porsche with a Düsseldorf tag. No, I didn't ask her yet. She's first-class, isn't she?"

I did not reply to the question but said: "I have an idea that the red notebook is hers. Go and ask her and come back and report to me. Then we will have an ice cream together and discuss the case in detail."

"OK, Chief," said Klaus, and started to leave. Then he turned around again and whispered, "Narcotics?"

He seemed disappointed when I could not confirm the suspicion.

"White slave trade?" he asked, somewhat less enthusiastic.

"Weapons!" I replied, in the same conspiratorial voice, and his face became radiant again. Whistling happily, he left.

Narcotics would have been better, but a detective has to be satisfied with whatever assignment he gets.

◎

My vacation was over.

My assumption was correct. The red notebook was the property of the girl in the bikini. From then on, Klaus and I paid her still more attention, though not exclusively toward her curves and the stretchability of her scanty swimsuit. We were more interested in her activities during the brief intervals she was not with the Italian—when she was sunbathing, playing badminton, or in her room. We noticed her asking at the reception desk for letters or cables, her occasional long-distance conversations with London, Rotterdam, Antwerp, and Liège, and the times when she handed the Porsche keys to her friend, sending him away, while she retired to the vacant writing room.

A week's observation gave me sufficient evidence for a binding case. The girl maintained a flourishing weapons business. I could not resist the temptation to extend the investigation further. Assisted by the number of her car tag and some very helpful and friendly connections with officers of the Criminal Investigation Bureau in several West German cities, I established the girl's identity and place of residence.

In addition, colleagues of mine in Brussels and Amsterdam were extremely helpful, and I also got help from a couple of writers for an economics journal in the Rhine-Ruhr section. What I got from them was really amazing.

Finally, I received a special-delivery letter from a good friend, an inspector of the Criminal Investigation Bureau, and this provided a big surprise.

In the end, she herself spoke to me.

The afternoon had been extremely hot and humid, and toward evening the air was so sultry that a thunderstorm seemed imminent. Alone in the lobby, I was leafing through my notes on the curvaceous blonde and her business associates, when the object of my interest strolled in.

Not three feet from my table, she suddenly stopped, turned around, and said calmly, pretending to be busy with her abbreviated clothing: "Good evening! I've noticed, with some surprise, that you seem to take a considerable interest in me."

"Is that really so surprising?" I replied.

She lifted her beautiful gray-blue eyes and said, after a long pause, "I think your interest concerns different objects from what the men here crane their necks for."

"I wouldn't say that." I tried to distract her again, but she did not believe me.

"Tell me honestly, please, what you are after!" she demanded.

I had to make a quick decision, and after hesitating briefly, I decided to tell her the truth. Without any reservations I told her the conclusions I had come to about her and, of course, about the little red book.

She turned pale under her suntan.

"May I sit down?" she whispered, and sank into a chair.

After she sipped some whiskey I had ordered, she regained her composure, and our conversation continued.

"What do you care about my business?" she asked. "Why don't you mind your own? How could you dare to expose my private life? Isn't there one spark of decency in you?"

If this were the beginning of my investigations, such a reproach might have impressed me. After all, I was on vacation and had no earthly reason to get involved in an affair that resulted from a red notebook found by a little boy. In fact, I was at first plagued by some scruples: I felt like a mean little man trying to look through keyholes to provide divorce evidence. All reporters experience such feelings from time to time.

However, in the blonde's case remorse was fleeting. The public was entitled to know about the secret million-dollar weapons deals, and the enormous profits that resulted in the slaughter of human beings. People ought to be told that an international crisis demands sacrifices from us all: For some it is only an increase in the cost of goods, which, because of panic, are hoarded and become more expensive; but for many others it means the loss of a husband or father called to war, not to mention those patriots who interrupt their lives and risk everything for an idea that in reality is only the fruit of a sales-promotion campaign by a few unscrupulous businessmen.

I explained all this, and more, to the young lady, who, because she was furious, looked even more attractive. She was in a rage, and when she shook her head her blonde hair fluttered, and at least the upper part of her bikini was seriously in danger of giving way to the strain.

Suddenly she jumped up. "I ought to have you killed!"

At that moment a thunderstorm erupted.

An enormous bolt of lightning struck the lake, followed by deafening thunder, and then, while lightning and thunder appeared to intermingle continuously, the clouds seemed to burst.

The young lady who had just wanted to have me killed suddenly changed her attitude.

She had endured the lightning, but the thunder that followed was too much for her. Her eyes wide with fear, her shaking hands tight against her ears, she pressed close to me for protection. The worst of the storm lasted about twenty minutes; then the thunder abated, and was finally drowned out by a steady downpour.

When she had regained some self-control, the blonde seemed somewhat embarrassed. After a few moments she said, "I'll tell you everything." She got up. "Please wait a few minutes. I'll get dressed and send Angelino out. I'll be back soon."

Angelino, the "little angel," apparently did not expect lengthy explanations, because she returned after about ten minutes, dressed casually in skirt, blouse, and a light sweater. She looked even more attractive now.

We ordered a drink, and suffering the—according to sex —indignant or envious glances of the other guests around us, began our conversation with some small talk.

After the last guests had left—the Dutch ladies and Klaus's

father, who could hardly contain his curiosity—the girl said abruptly, "You know who I am and where I come from, but do you also know the circumstances that caused me to lead a, let's say, unusual life?"

I hesitated to reply. It was true: I knew her identity. She was not about twenty-five, as I had at first assumed, but close to thirty, came from an aristocratic East Prussian family, and could command the title "Countess." I knew also that she had lived in West Germany since 1946. The aforementioned special delivery letter contained the details of how she had then, at seventeen, survived. But I was determined to let sleeping dogs lie. I suspected that I was about to be entertained with a sentimental tale.

She seemed to guess my thoughts.

"I'll spare you the details," she said sarcastically, "but you must permit me to go back a little." She lighted a cigarette and began her story.

Her parents had been divorced. At the beginning of World War II, her father was drafted and was killed in Poland. She lived with an aunt, a princess, at their mansion in Küstrin near the Baltic Sea. There she had a governess from the French-speaking part of Switzerland who was responsible for her education. When she had just turned fifteen, in the winter of 1944, the Russian-German front line came very close, but this was more or less ignored at the mansion. On the day that she was to travel with her governess to distant relatives in Bavaria, the Russian Army made a breakthrough that overran the estate.

"No, what you think did not happen," she said; and added sarcastically: "Perhaps it would sound better if I said I had been raped. But it's not true. A very nice Russian captain prevented it, and I became his girl friend. At the end of May— my captain had long departed and left me to a fellow officer—the staff quarters, located in our mansion, moved to Potsdam. I accompanied my officer, but this caused him trouble. He took me to Berlin, gave me some money, and promised to take care of me. I never saw him again."

She continued her story in the same objective tone. After a brief and sad interlude with a sergeant from American headquarters, she fell into the hands of an Englishman who, at first, took no notice of the teen-ager's charm, but employed her for the sale of cigarettes on Berlin's black market. During the winter of 1945 she became acquainted with the French occupation force. Because of her French-speaking governess, she was fluent in French, and therefore considered worthy to dust the office of a silver-haired French colonel; given the title of "personal interpreter," she was also occasionally requested to sweeten his nights.

This promising career, which could have led her into the arms of a three-star general, came to a sudden end when a large sum of money was found to be missing from the colonel's safe. The money was the hard-earned proceeds from the sale of a considerable number of travel permits to East German refugees who wanted to move to the Western sectors—approximately $60,000. The countess was suspected, and the colonel had her arrested. She was interrogated by the military police, but when no evidence could be found against her she was thrown into the streets. She went to see her friend, the black marketeer, to ask for her half of the booty he held in custody, but he only laughed. Because he was a decent fellow—after all, he had been an officer and was also an aristocrat—he gave her a carton of American cigarettes before he told her to go to hell.

Assisted by this precious merchandise and her by now internationally proved charm, she transferred to the West, to Hanover, first in the company of a truck driver, then in the big American car of a diamond buyer from Antwerp. The trade she would begin during her six-week stay with the diamond merchant would later be of great benefit to her. However, her odyssey ended almost where it began—a princely château.

There the young countess was given a friendly welcome by her deceased aunt's distant relatives, and trusted as one of their own urgently in need of care.

"They behaved as if just the day before I had been to dancing lessons in Küstrin, and had lost home and family by fire, flood, or by any other cruel fate," the blonde said sarcastically.

"War and Germany's collapse, the Russian occupation and the wild months immediately after the war, these catastrophes were ignored completely. I was treated like a teen-ager, encouraged to do embroidery and play the piano, and sent twice a month to the next small town for a visit to the beauty salon, with an old governess as chaperone."

So she lived until Christmas, 1946.

Then one of the pious old ladies who were abundant at the château surprised her one night when she sneaked out of the groom's quarters to go back to her maidenly room.

At first, this caused a dreadful scandal and a lot of embarrassing questions; then it seemed to dawn on her uncles and aunts that eighteen months among soldiers and adventurers might leave their traces even on a countess brought up in the strict Prussian discipline. It was decided to handle her delicate case with the utmost discretion.

The groom was fired, but received an excellent "certificate of service." The countess, equipped with warm recommendations and some money, was sent to southern Germany where she would be given a new start in life with other relatives—perhaps she could study music or art there.

In January, 1947, she traveled to Bavaria and was to begin rounds of relatives' châteaux there, not as the teen-ager needing protection, but as an independent young lady traveling to complete her studies.

From time to time she explained to her hosts that she had to journey to the Munich library or to settle a problem regarding her registration at the university. In these instances, she was put on the train, given all sorts of messages and recommendations and the addresses of some aristocratic landladies. Sometimes she was asked to make some little purchases: a pound of coffee, some cigarettes, or a bottle of liqueur. Everyone pretended that these items were staple commodities—not black-market goods obtainable only through trade-ins of appropriate value. She was given some small pieces of jewelry to exchange for such rarities.

There were gold cuff links, bearing the family coat of
arms, that had been worn by a nephew who had died at Stalin-
grad, Mama's old-fashioned diamond brooch, and some gold-
plated ice spoons. But nothing was mentioned of how these
treasures were converted into coffee or cigarettes. Presumably,
the countess was expected to carry out an illegal transaction
or, even worse, do something that was not in accordance with
the high code of honor of her class.

Owing to etiquette, she obliged without revealing the
methods she applied in dealing with the Möhlstrasse black
marketeers. Her Berlin experiences proved to be valuable, and
most of the time she returned with more than her relatives and
friends expected to get.

Word of her ability was passed around the widely
branched-out family; and soon the countess, still an ardent art
student, became a specialist in the conversion of gold and precious jewelry owned by the old established aristocracy, including
salvaged treasures of the nobility among the refugees from the
East who had found shelter with wealthy relatives.

The old countesses and baronesses who, before the arrival
of the Russian Army, had hidden their treasure chests in the
grooms' quarters and later brought them across the Elbe River
to the West spoke with benevolent smiles of the charming little
countess who tried to utilize her "inborn self-possession" and
"really superb conduct" to everyone's benefit. They did not
know—or want to know—that her knowledge of precious stones
derived from her hotel-room experiences with a diamond buyer,
that the haggling and shrewdness came from living in the ruins
around a bombed-out Berlin railroad station, and that her self-
confidence with men of every age group did not stem from her
aristocratic background, but was the result of the rough experience she had gained in the beds of soldiers and civilians of at
least six nations.

All these minor and not so minor transactions continued
to everyone's satisfaction until two new factors emerged: a
Rumanian with a highly developed instinct for new talent and

opportunity who took the young countess under his wing, and the arrival in Bavaria of a new wave of refugees, bringing some highly aristocratic ladies equipped with particularly magnificent jewelry to the châteaux and mansions of Bavaria.

A few weeks later the countess, now seventeen years of age, presented the first jewels to her Rumanian lover, who was about thirty years her senior: diamond earclips with two-carat stones and a three-carat solitaire and three brooches with emeralds, diamonds, and rubies.

He said something that would have been fashionable as an expression of highest appreciation in his home town of Arad during the early twenties, but she did not share his enthusiasm.

"The stones are hot," she said coolly. "We won't be able to sell them at Möhlstrasse; there we could only expect that a captain from the Midwest would exchange them for cigarettes. I think you should have rings made from them and I will then try to sell them to our advantage to some GI's who are not quite dry behind their ears."

Soon word got around the American troops that a poor Hungarian count, with his pretty fun-loving daughter, had moved into a Munich suburb, and a small gift, a carton of cigarettes, or a bottle of Bourbon perhaps, would be most welcome there. The count not only was careless of his daughter's virtue but would also part with rings adorned with precious stones and heraldic figures cheap.

Faultless blue-white diamonds from the diadems and necklaces belonging to the ladies of nobility went another way. They were sold by the countess, for fantastically high amounts of "old marks," to emigrants tired of Europe. She would return the jewelry to their owners after her Rumanian had replaced the first-class stones with others of inferior value. "The offers I received weren't high enough," she would say in such cases on returning the looted jewelry, and she put the sighing ladies off to another time.

On two occasions there was trouble: An old countess noticed the exchange of her choice diamonds for third-class stones, and protested so vehemently that the countess had to dig deep into her pockets to protect her reputation. She returned to Munich immediately and brought back $25,000 and the explanation that she had threatened to sue the swindling merchant if he refused to pay ample compensation or buy the necklace for its true value. The old countess, deeply moved by so much honesty, gave up the inferior necklace for her to return to the penitent merchant, with a reward of $2,500 for the young countess's diligence in handling the matter.

The young countess refused the money indignantly, because she could very well afford the loss of $2,500. Her reputation among the aristocracy was more important.

The second time she was in trouble was when the Munich Vice Squad requested her registration as a prostitute. She had a narrow escape thanks to the invention of a particularly clever and sentimental story, and the energetic intervention by the senior of one of the oldest South German aristocratic families, which had many high government officials and prelates among them.

She left the Rumanian, who, after her departure, discovered the loss of nearly $20,000 and more than an additional $125,000 in marks. He expressed his sorrow in a most unaristocratic manner.

And because she was a serious and thorough girl, she also took a suitcase filled with gold and jewels, which the Rumanian had either bought or held on consignment. She notified the owners of all such jewelry that a merchant whom she had fully trusted had disappeared, together with the jewels—foul play, murder, or kidnapping, was suspected, perhaps by a member of the occupation army. In any event, to avoid involvement with the United States Military Police, it was inadvisable to pursue the matter.

She threatened the Rumanian with about forty paragraphs of the German Penal Law and with the very sensitive consciences of the judges of the United States Criminal Court, who would have no mercy with pimping, selling and buying of occupation currency or with receiving stolen property belonging to the Allied Forces.

After she had satisfactorily rearranged her young life and considerably increased her fortune, she bedded with the nearly senile aristocrat who had earlier snatched her from the jaws of the Munich Vice Squad.

By the time she celebrated her eighteenth birthday in the company of her aged admirer and the leaders of the old and new society, currency reform had come into effect. She suffered only minor losses because, counseled by her benefactor, she had invested her considerable holdings in real estate and industrial stocks.

Thereafter she lived only for pleasure, apart from a short period of mourning for her deceased benefactor. But she soon realized that not even a formidable fortune could withstand continuous extravagant spending.

When she was nearly twenty, she decided to use her remaining capital for a new start that could immediately provide her with the carefree life of a multimillionaire. She made some fruitless attempts to import narcotics, with the idea of establishing her own sales organization to work the mid-European market. Her efforts failed because of the watchfulness of Interpol and the new German Federal Police.

A cautious trial partnership in a ring that stole automobiles quickly proved to be a mistake.

She was favorably impressed by a proposal made soon afterward by a casual acquaintance, a tall, broad-shouldered, suntanned gentleman with conspicuous gray temples and keen, gray-green eyes.

At the time of their meeting he called himself Roy Fitzgerald; when he departed this world two years later, in the Bay of Tonkin, mortally wounded by a machine-gun burst, his friends and customers mourned for him as Danny McCloy. Whatever his name, during his lifetime he was one of the most successful gun- and blockade-runners on the South China coast. Although his prices included an extra 300 percent margin, he always found consumers not only with a big demand but also with lots of cash.

Roy introduced the countess to the weapons traffic. He had come to Europe for a brief visit to explore new sources of supply, and the advice he gave her was completely unselfish.

"You're just as capable as our other European suppliers," he said. "And there's no risk involved here, not like the kind we run when we take the stuff through the blockades."

With the contempt of a frontline soldier for those behind the lines, he initiated her into the private practices and tricks of the weapons trade, later introducing her to some of the well-known merchants to gain practical experience.

The gentlemen to whom Roy Fitzgerald introduced the young countess were all successful weapons dealers of widely varying backgrounds. For example, she met an elderly Scandinavian who devoured her with his eyes, and immediately offered her the management of one of his branch offices. His name was J. J. Petersen.

The next was an Italian movie director, an eager and corpulent little man, one of Petersen's friends who claimed to have large quantities of well-preserved infantry rifles in his warehouses.

She met American officers, administrators of United States Army depots in Germany, who offered a variety of weapons. She came upon gentlemen from Prague wearing exquisitely tailored suits made from the very best English worsted materials, who offered, on behalf of a socialist, government-owned agency called Omnipol, immense quantities of weapons. She encountered a Bulgarian hotel porter who had immigrated to Frankfurt and who claimed to have excellent connections with custodians of old German weapons depots in the Balkans.

And she was introduced to fellow aristocrats who had been successful in the weapons trade, for example, a count residing in Munich, but she was not interested in renewing her acquaintance with aristocratic South German families. (In this particular case, a Von Bodirsky from Vienna acted as the count's middleman, and promised immediate delivery of any quantity of infantry weapons and ammunition at favorable rates.) But the countess preferred to do business with the robust type, even if they were customers, provided they were successful and had a modicum of manners.

Two gentlemen of Roy Fitzgerald's acquaintance impressed her most: an immaculately groomed, middle-aged German, Hans Joachim Seidenschnur, and a merry, hard-drinking Norwegian, Rolf Ragnar Lie.

A toast:
Rolf Ragnar Lie and associate, celebrating
the sale of 40 tons of TNT.

Photo: Collection Bernt Engelmann

After a brief deliberation, the countess chose to associate with the Norwegian, who appeared to be the director of a Cologne armaments company, Gustav Genschow & Co. GmbH, a subsidiary of the Flick Syndicate.

During the following months she traveled with him through Europe, promoting their common business interests with vigor and diligence. After successfully concluding an enormous ammunition transaction involving herself, Lie, Genschow & Co., and also a certain Georg Puchert, alias Captain Morris, she retired with Lie to a magnificent château at Lago Maggiore, and when Lie, intimidated by the Red Hand, repeatedly resorted to the aquavit bottle, she took charge of the business alone. Since that time she conducted several amusing and lucrative transactions. By far the most ironic one was during the Suez crisis, with the United States providing most of the profits.

However, the initial phase of the amusing Suez business was deadly serious. When in the fall of 1956, British, French, and Israeli forces launched a combined attack toward the Suez Canal Zone and the Sinai Peninsula, the Soviet Union immediately promised weapons to the Egyptians. At the last moment, the Russians decided to make a slight change: Instead of factory-new Russian rifles, bazookas, and machine guns, the shipment consisted of a variety of foreign arms. This would be less embarrassing should the weapons be captured by the enemy. But where could they be obtained in time? Russian emissaries explored the European market hurriedly, and grasped the opportunity when the countess offered Finnish howitzers, Belgian carbines and machine guns, Swiss antitank guns, and a few bazookas of alleged British origin—all ready and waiting for shipment in the free port of Trieste.

The Russians did not barter long, and the next day the weapons were loaded onto a fortuitously available Russian freighter. During the journey to Alexandria, the crates were provided with Russian inscriptions—the Egyptians would see who would come to their aid in an hour of emergency! Just before the British-French-Israeli attack on Egypt, the weapons arrived in Alexandria and were transferred immediately onto waiting trucks for dispatch to the Sinai front, arriving there just in time to be unloaded and assembled for use against the expected Israeli attack in this sector.

A few hours later, the Egyptian Army was destroyed by the Israelis, and the Russian crates of weapons for the Sinai front were captured by the victorious Israeli forces.

They had no use for them; they did not know what to do with the enormous booty of weapons and equipment from all over the world.

They happily accepted the offer of an American firm to buy all the captured weapons en bloc and to take care of the transportation problem. Among the enormous quantities of weapons, ammunition, and equipment that found their way from the holds of huge freighters to warehouses in the port of New York were crated weapons the countess had sold to the Russians for shipment to Egypt.

Of course, the Americans noticed the Russian inscriptions when they inspected the crates more closely.

"Original Russian weapons crates," one of the inspectors said thoughtfully. "That could be something for Intelligence."

Several inconspicuous gentlemen quickly arrived from Washington and inspected the still unopened crates bearing Russian markings.

"We'll open one of the crates as a test case," they said. Only by chance did they open a crate that contained bazookas the countess had claimed originated from England but proved to be original Russian weapons in original Russian wrappings. The men from Washington were delighted.

Several months later, the crates reappeared—this time during an American press conference at the SEATO High Command in Southeast Asia.

The United States tried to furnish evidence for Russian interference in a local conflict that threatened to expand into a dangerous crisis. For this purpose the same weapons crates were displayed for the press. The liaison officer was to read a long statement; then the crates would be opened.

As it was very hot, and because there was not much time left to cable reports for inclusion in the weekend edition of American and European newspapers—reporting the discovery of Russian arms with the Southeast Asian rebels—only one crate was opened. It contained the original Russian bazookas, in original Russian wrappings. And thus the United States was spared great embarrassment, because all the other crates on display were filled with weapons from Belgium, Finland, and Switzerland.

The American propaganda victory later proved to be justified: Two weeks after the press conference, which was somewhat manipulated, of course, genuine Russian weapons were captured from the jungle guerrillas in the Southeast Asian trouble spot.

"You will remember," she said, concluding her story, "that I sold the weapons in Trieste to the Russians. They were then shipped to the Egyptians, captured by the Israelis, bought by a United States firm and sold to the CIA, who made them reappear in Southeast Asia as 'evidence' for Russian interference. But from whom did I at first buy the weapons?" When I looked at her, uncomprehending, she drew languidly on her cigarette, and continued: "I had bought them cheap from a firm that had difficulties with loading in Trieste for one reason or another and wanted to sell in a hurry—a United States firm, the same, by the way, that bought the crates back after the Sinai attack. It is such a large organization that the left hand didn't know what the right hand was doing. They have worldwide branches, their own numerous factories, and headquarters in Salzburg, Austria. Their name is—"

"—International Armament Corporation!" I interrupted.

"Correct," the countess said, "and with this same firm I have just completed my most profitable deal, which will make it possible for me to retire."

My expression must have been incredulous, because the bikini girl definitely did not appear to be a tired, graying businesswoman awaiting retirement.

"Well," she corrected herself, "maybe I don't want to retire, but I intend to get married."

"Angelino?" I inquired politely.

She made a contemptuous gesture. "Oh, come now," she said. "He's only a silly boy, a casual interlude."

"Director Lie?"

"He's finished," said the countess, and though her words sounded brutal, it was true. A hopeless alcoholic, he died a few months later of a liver disease.

"Maybe the lucky man is Seidenschnur?" I inquired.

The countess disagreed. "He's a man I could like a lot," she added. "But I have far more ambitious plans. I'm thinking of a really serious union. After all, I can afford it! I'm sure you know the man in question; he is a banker and a leading economics expert, and therefore I cannot reveal his name. He is acquainted with ministers, ambassadors, and generals, on the board of directors of more than a dozen organizations; the most influential government officials are his fraternity brothers, and he is nearly as wealthy as I."

"Does he also traffic in weapons?" I took the liberty to ask.

I expected to be reprimanded, but she replied: "He has a hand in the armaments business, of course, but he is interested only in sizable transactions. And because he has excellent connections, and we intend to be married, I included him in the profits of my last major sale on a 5 percent basis."

Her reference to "sizable transactions" had me very curious, and finally I asked her about it.

The countess smiled. "I'd like to suggest a little exchange agreement," she said, after a brief pause. "If I appear in your report anonymously so that my marriage plans will not be affected, I'll introduce you to the world's greatest living weapons merchant, the new Zaharoff."

I did not ponder long.

After all, my main purpose was to gather information about the weapons traffic, and I regarded my subject as endemic to our society; the people involved were important only with regard to their backgrounds, their motives and methods. It never was (nor is it) my intention to be a judge of morals. My duty is to be a reporter.

And when I have the opportunity to broaden my reporting by forfeiting some minor details, the choice is easy.

"Well," the countess asked impatiently, "can I remain anonymous, and do you want to meet the new Zaharoff?"

Not long ago she had wanted to have me killed. Then she had tried to convince me of her feminine helplessness during a thunderstorm. Now, cool and composed, she suggested a deal.

If I did not upset her plan to be accepted by the *crème de la crème* of West German society by marrying the influential director of a bank, she would reveal the real tycoon, the man who was pulling the strings behind the scenes.

How could I turn down such an offer?

THE MAN
IN THE SHADOW

THE COUNTESS HAD MENTIONED the *new* Zaharoff, but first I needed some information about the *old* Zaharoff. All I knew was that at the turn of the century he had acquired a legendary reputation as an international weapons dealer and had then influenced world politics through his immense power and wealth.

To obtain objective information on the "man in the shadow" turned out to be a difficult task. It was obvious that some of Zaharoff's biographers had been hired only for the purpose of whitewashing him. Other publications were aimed at public relations, and still others preached blind hatred against the "Levantine weapons smuggler," and were grossly exaggerated, distorting the historic truth.

On the following points all biographers agreed:

The "man in the shadow" was born as Zacharias Basileios Zacharoff on October 6, 1849, in the Turkish community of Muğla, and he died on November 27, 1936, eighty-seven years old, in Monte Carlo, Monaco, as Sir Basil Zaharoff.

During his last years as a member of the British aristocracy and high financial circles, his interest in the weapons business had faded slightly. But he still made loans to the Balkan countries, mainly Rumania, participated in the various enterprises sponsored by the Anglo-Persian Oil Company, operated (like, much later, his compatriot Onassis) the Monte Carlo Casino, and was so much carried away by goodness that, apart from the usual contributions, he established several nonprofit charitable funds for the benefit of poor citizens of his native country, members of the Christian faith.

However, their number was somewhat limited because, despite the fact that there were many poor people in Muğla, the Turks had murdered the majority of the Christian Greeks, and the survivors of the massacre were forced to leave. Therefore, the number of people qualified to receive benefits from the aged millionaire's charitable fund was comparatively small, the per capita amount for each Greek beggar of the Christian faith was exceptionally high, and the praise by those who received Zaharoff's alms was extremely loud.

But even the small sum—compared with his income—Zaharoff contributed for the benefit of the Christian poor of his birthplace was still more than his *own* starting capital. (The reader is to give special attention to the word "own," and shall soon see why.)

During the anti-Greek riots the Zaharoffs were forced to leave Muğla, found shelter with rich relatives in Constantinople, and from then on lived off the family's generosity.

When little Basileios turned fifteen, the family council decided that it was time he worked for his own support. He was apprenticed to a rich uncle, a merchant.

Most rich uncles are stingy, but it could also be that only stingy uncles get rich. In any event, the uncle kept Basileios short of cash, so short, in fact, that the nephew had to resort to a little sideline business if he ever wanted the feel of a piaster in his hands. And because this desire was very strong, he used the hours during which other boys slept, the only spare time the uncle left him, to act as a guide for foreigners and wealthy visitors from the provinces out on a night in Constantinople. He procured whatever they desired, soon had agreements with nightclubs and hotels, and accumulated, apart from a mounting income, a wide knowledge of human nature and the seamier side of life. He also learned what he could of foreign languages and all sorts of artifices. During the day, in his uncle's business, he learned the good old Levantine trade customs and secrets. In this way he received the benefit of an all-around education, which would prove exceedingly valuable in his later enterprise: dealing in weapons. Strictly speaking, he should have been grateful to his uncle, but this was not so.

After about three years he came to the conclusion that his uncle had exploited him long enough. While his wealthy uncle was on a business trip to Odessa, Basileios decided it was time for a change. And as he had seen enough of Constantinople, he started the search for a new job in London.

In order to have some help for his new start in life, he took a considerable amount of money from his uncle's safe. There are two versions about the legitimacy of this deed: The first is by Zaharoff's uncle, who sent two of the cleverest Levantine lawyers after him to London, accusing him of common robbery. The second version originates with Zaharoff himself, stating that he was his uncle's partner, and consequently entitled to take an appropriate share for his toil. By sheer coincidence, this was just the amount reposing in his uncle's safe.

Attempts to determine the lawful owner of the cash were futile. Basil, as he now called himself, had the money, and his uncle had the trouble. He had his nephew arrested, and Basil was briefly imprisoned before being brought before Old Bailey Criminal Court. The money was not found, and Basil Zaharoff was acquitted for lack of evidence.

However, this short time in prison destroyed the young man's fanciful plans. He had intended to buy a partnership in an English merchant house, but who would accept a young Levantine just released from jail? Resignedly, but considerably wealthier, Zaharoff traveled east, not to his native country, Turkey, fearing that his London acquittal might not be accepted there, but to the home of all Greeks, Athens.

Of course, Athenians are sensitive regarding strict adherence to the rules of mercantile honor, but not oversensitive. After all, Athens is not only the home of the classic philosopher, but the metropolis of the Balkans. But if a young man appears from nearby Constantinople, cursed by his honorable uncle as thief of his till, announced from faraway London as an adventurer and jailbird, respectable Athenian businessmen would hesitate to get mixed up with him. Their doors are kept closed to such strangers in Greece, because there are enough native thiefs with whose tricks one is familiar.

Making progress in Athens was difficult for Basil Zaharoff. Only a few lonesome widows trying to retain their youth derived any pleasure from his visits.

And then, just when his traveling money from Constantinople was low and he still had not found a satisfactory position, came his opportunity. A British-Swedish armaments organization of modest stature was searching for an agile young man, completely familiar with the customs of the Balkan countries, the Levant, and the Middle East, a representative who was shrewd, possessed good manners and few scruples, who would keep expenses down, but make good profits for his employers. Nobody wanted the job but Basil Zaharoff.

He harassed and begged an influential but sentimental Greek politician—the only one he had been able to contact—to recommend him for the job.

"He speaks English reasonably well," Zaharoff's supporter finished his somewhat lame report on the qualities of his charge. This was the decisive point.

Pleased to have found an agile Greek with whom they could converse, the board of directors appointed Zaharoff as their general representative for the sale of guns and ammunition for the Balkans-Levant territory.

It was fortunate for the new representative of British-Swedish arms manufacturers that a war should break out in the Balkans during the first weeks of his new appointment. The "Czar-Liberator" of Russia attempted to free the Bulgarians from Turkish slavery in order to get them under his own yoke. The whole of the Balkans went into a war psychosis, considerably promoting the sale of arms.

Of course, Zaharoff had competition: The sales representatives of the large trusts like Vickers and Armstrong, Schneider-Creusot and Krupp were very active, and so, too, were the salesmen of Spanish, Italian, Austrian, and Swiss organizations.

The methods applied by these competitors were not always delicate, but at least they had scruples. Even a veteran armaments salesman would hesitate before trying to sneak a five-digit check to a defense minister in the presence of the Parliamentary Control Commission. But hesitation was not for Zaharoff.

He was in a great hurry to get into business, and he had nothing to lose. He would not have been too timid to put bags of gold pieces on the minister's desk, even in the presence of the district attorney dedicated to suppressing corruption.

He succeeded in getting a foothold in the Balkans, and his employers in London and Stockholm began to respect their eager Eastern representative, and looked forward to his amazing orders.

Zaharoff's competitors operated from the conservative viewpoint that the cheapest offer had the best prospect of being accepted. Zaharoff applied the opposite method: He offered his guns for twice the competition's price, and slipped the politicians deciding the sales three times more in bribes than his competitors would dare to offer. Even ministers only moderately literate know arithmetic: 30 percent of two million is six times as much as 10 percent of one million. They therefore demanded 40 percent of two and a half million, and Zaharoff got the order. There were many more orders, because the boom continued.

Peace would not be restored in the Balkans for a long time. When a country appeared tired of war, sometimes even moderate bribes were sufficient to remedy the situation and bring on a new crisis. A few thousand gold francs paid to the editor of a normally peace-loving newspaper, a few hundred leva to a

border guard who had never before fired a shot—and a new
incident was created. The parliaments approved new armaments
credits; the ministerial offices allocated—for still higher percentages of still higher-priced bids—new orders for weapons.

But when a country buys arms, its neighbors have to be
careful. Zaharoff was one of the first to realize the unlimited
opportunities of an armaments race. When he had succeeded,
for example, in selling a new miracle weapon like a submarine
to the Greek Navy and the second one of the same type to
Rumania, he considered it an unpatriotic act and somewhat im-
moral to sell the next three submarines to the mortal enemies of
these two customers, namely, the Turkish Navy, but he always
had the strength to overcome such reservations.

He received huge orders, from which his company made
considerable profits, and expanded his territory: The Hapsburg
monarchy, the Russian Czarist Empire, and even faroff Spain
were visited by him and included in his sales.

In Russia he was the darling of the young Imperial Guard
officers for whom he gave extravagant parties. Word got around
the Imperial Court, and soon there were elderly gentlemen—all
very influential and important for the allocation of arms contracts—eager to participate in the benefits Zaharoff offered. In
Spain he enjoyed the favor of the Royal Court and the ministerial offices through a lady friend who paved the way for him,
arranged for the audiences he desired, and thwarted his competitors. The lady was the Duchess of Villafranca, the young
wife of an influential Spanish nobleman.

In Austria he employed a different method. When an
American inventor named Maxim appeared in Vienna with a
sensational new weapon—a small quick-firing gun—Zaharoff
boldly gave a press conference and explained to the journalists
who had been kept ignorant of this military secret that the new
gun was a product of his employers.

The bluff deprived Maxim of a contract he was almost
certain to obtain: Maxim was forced to sell all his rights to
Zaharoff's London-based employers for a small partnership in

the company. Only a few days earlier the Austrian Government had requested the identity of the manufacturer and had been brazenly told the gun could be supplied only through Zaharoff.

Zaharoff's relationship with the British-Swedish organization had also undergone some slight changes. The capable Greek, who was no longer a youth, had advanced to a partnership, and it would not be long before he would become the head of the organization that now strove to advance from a medium-sized armaments manufacture to the front line of the giant weapons trusts.

During the years before the outbreak of World War I, the organization's name was changed to Vickers & Maxim, and their general representative and principal stockholder was Basil Zaharoff.

The comparatively small Balkans and Levant business, which had brought Zaharoff from financial strife to considerable wealth, was from now on of secondary importance—obscured by a tenfold bigger business resulting from the arms race between the Entente Cordiale and the German-Austrian alliance.

The extent of Zaharoff's responsibility for World War I will never be known. However, he had his hand in everything. When newspapers demanded a fresh and lusty war, more *Lebensraum,* or only bloody revenge, there was Zaharoff as instigator and profiteer. When British, German, French, or Russian armaments trusts fought their internal and external battles, or established secret alliances—a not too infrequent occurrence—Zaharoff helped pull the strings. After the Russo-Japanese War, in which Russia was deplorably defeated, the Russian giant was built up to become one of the biggest military powers on earth. Credits and loans were granted, and when Krupp and Schneider-Creusot, Skoda and Blohm & Voss extended and modernized the Russian armaments industry, it was Zaharoff who brought it off and in the end secured the lion's share for himself and Vickers-Maxim.

And when, on July 28, 1914, World War I, the war so badly desired by the armaments industry, became a reality, when in Berlin the cry "Now we will beat them" sounded, and when in Paris peace-loving Jean Jaurès was murdered, France awarded Basil Zaharoff the title "Commander of the Legion of Honor"—for outstanding services.

World War I ran its course, taking the lives of millions; causing unimaginable destruction; violently shaking the foundations of the victorious powers as well as of the defeated; destroying three empires and changing the social structure of most civilized countries. But, for Zaharoff, World War I brought high honors, and his influence increased tremendously.

He became a multimillionaire, was knighted by the King of England, received the highest orders of merit and—an ironic joke—was appointed adviser to the British Prime Minister for peace negotiations in Versailles, Saint-Germain, and at the Grand Trianon. Sir Basil Zaharoff, holder of an honorary doctor's degree from Oxford University, Commander of the Legion of Honor, Knight of the Order of Bath, an adviser for peace negotiations! He whose worst enemy was peace!

New areas to feed his gigantic arms empire were explored: Poland, Lithuania, and the Ukraine, where armies against the advancing Bolsheviks were formed; Greece, which again armed itself against Turkey; and Morocco, Kurdistan, and other trouble spots. Sudden crises and small wars—old Zaharoff, seventy by now, needed them to keep the huge armies alert and to prevent their demobilization.

Some of his competitors, particularly Krupp, had disappeared from the international market through the Versailles Peace Treaty, and the big trusts in the Allied countries showed a tendency to merge. Soon the few really big syndicates controlled the market; their influence became even stronger; and they could apply their artifices once again to hurl a world tired of war into new crises and conflicts.

No one knew the art better than old Zaharoff.

He continued the game he had mastered with so much virtuosity for a few more years until he grew tired of it. Then Fate struck and finished his activities.

As it happens every so often, his decline began with a final triumph. In 1924, the then seventy-five-year-old weapons merchant could finally marry the only woman who had ever meant anything to him: the Duchess of Villafranca, his old benefactress at the Spanish Court, herself close to seventy. She had been widowed about six months earlier. But soon after the marriage, conducted with the utmost secrecy, Lady Zaharoff became severely ill. The old couple moved to the French Riviera, hoping to find relief in the mild climate, but a year later Lady Zaharoff died, and the old man received a severe blow. He who had negotiated the death of millions for over sixty years without batting an eye was heartbroken. He suffered a physical collapse, retired from the weapons business, and left his usual surroundings. He moved to a suite in the world-famous Hôtel de Paris in Monte Carlo, a suite that was then completely closed off from the rest of the hotel.

And because his love of money was ultimately greater than his sorrow, he acquired sufficient stock for a controlling interest in the Monte Carlo gambling casino across from the Hôtel de Paris, which yielded up to 100 percent dividends per year. Besides, he gambled a bit with his millions—but of course not at the roulette or baccarat table. Zaharoff had only contempt for such small risks. Instead he speculated in oil in Persia and Rumania, and won again.

Apparently this gave him renewed courage to take to the field again. But this time his eyes were closed to reality. He took an unprecedented risk.

Without any guaranty, without backing, and perhaps for the first time without selfish motives, he poured millions upon millions into an undertaking that even in the event of success would have little prospects for profit. He tried to liberate the Greeks in Asia Minor from Turkish rule.

The attempt was a failure, militarily and politically. Economically it was a fiasco. The Venizelos government, very friendly with Zaharoff, collapsed; the liberation army equipped (on credit) by Zaharoff suffered a crushing defeat by the Turks, and one and a half million Greeks living in Zaharoff's home territory fled Asia Minor in wild panic. They left behind not only their worldly possessions but also thousands of victims of the Turk's fury incited by Zaharoff's money.

Zaharoff, who had not left Monte Carlo during these events, said, "I don't want to hear any more of the Greeks' affairs."

Nor did he want to be bothered with anything anymore, especially questions. A bitter old man, confined to a wheelchair, he lived in deep seclusion. After a lifetime of bribing the press, he now detested reporters.

Guarded by private detectives, his waning years were spent on the balcony of the Hôtel de Paris under the eternally blue sky of the Côte d'Azur. No one could come near him but a servant, who brought him from his bedroom to the balcony and, late in the evenings, back to the bedroom, served his meals, and occasionally announced a visitor. Zaharoff might give a brief moment to his closest confidants; strangers never had a chance to see him.

When a French reporter tried to force an interview by hinting at an affair that was particularly embarrassing to Zaharoff, and thus far unknown to the public, the servant returned the card on which the reporter had written his indiscreet hint.

Under it was written, in Zaharoff's hand: *"M. Zaharoff, n'ayant pas de voix, ne peut pas chanter."* (As Mr. Zaharoff has no voice, he cannot sing.) It should be noted that *faire chanter* in French means "make to sing," that is, submit to blackmail.

When Basil Zaharoff at eighty-seven died in his wheelchair on the balcony of the Hôtel de Paris on November 27, 1936, he could afford a final cynical smile. He took most of his secrets to the grave with him and he had enjoyed his millions derived from inflamed passions and wars, which gave him his titles, degrees, and every possible luxury—and an impenetrable shell from which curses rebounded.

What would I find when I visited the "new Zaharoff," the mysterious head of the International Armament Corporation?

Would I have the same experience as the French reporter thirty years ago who sought an interview with the greatest merchant of the era? Perhaps the countess was only having fun with me?

Though I tried to imagine what it would be like, I could only visualize a reception by an arrogant butler at the entrance of the Interarmco boss's presidential château, and then after a long wait in a gloomy hall, between a knight's armor and stuffed vultures, I would politely be asked to leave: "Mr. President regrets he has no voice today; he cannot sing."

But things turned out quite differently.

After my study of Zaharoff, I suggested to the countess that I might see only an old servant, not the old Interarmco head himself. She burst out laughing. Since our discussion a few nights ago, she had changed back to the carefree girl-in-the-bikini, passing the time with her red Porsche, the curly-haired Angelino, and lounging in the sun.

"You'll be surprised," she said, still laughing.

She was right.

Three days later it finally happened.

The mailman handed me a letter from Salzburg. The envelope and notepaper, of the highest quality, carried the Interarmco coat of arms and "Office of the President" tastefully embossed, and the elegant, typed message made my heart beat fast.

The President of the International Armament Corporation, Mr. Samuel Cummings, said the letter, would receive me at his Salzburg head office and would be prepared to provide whatever I desired.

This most welcome letter was signed by Ernst Werner Glatt, Vice President.

"Give the old boys my regards!" said the countess when I bade her farewell. "Don't irritate the bodyguards before you are on good terms with the boss, and don't forget: They are the biggest and most successful weapons dealers of our time. Very smart businessmen—despite their age!"

After I left the countess, I traveled directly to Salzburg. To my imagined mansion equipped with knights' armor, silver-

The shining example:
king of the weapons merchants, Sir Basil Zaharoff.

Photo: Historisches Bildarchiv Handke, Berneck

haired servants, and an ancient tycoon sitting on his balcony, wrapped in blankets, I added some details: Among the ironclad knights I could see broad-shouldered men in elegant custom-tailored suits, with shoulder-holstered guns, cleaning their teeth with solid-gold toothpicks, scratching their cauliflower ears, and ready to shoot anyone attempting to extinguish the last spark of life remaining in their leader.

Only when the white-starched uniformed nurse passed them with a glass of vegetable juice for the great old man on the balcony would their eyes show some lively interest, following her undulating hip movements.

On the wind-protected balcony, two very old Americans—the leader Sam Cummings and his vice president Glatt—would be playing poker, reviving their memories of the good old times during the Chinese civil war, the uprising in Kurdistan, or Abd-el-Kader's rebellion, and trying to cheat each other with little tricks and bluffs.

At intervals the nurse would bring a small solid-gold telephone and say, "This gentleman could not be sent away—he needs 20,000 infantry rifles before the end of the month, CIF Puerto Limón."

And then the old tycoon would take the receiver with a trembling hand and, after some short, tough bargaining, promise delivery.

Before continuing the poker game, he would say to his loyal deputy, "Call Holland and tell them to have 20,000 pieces ready on the 17th."

And his vice president would answer humbly, "Right, boss—will do!"

So it is with fantasies—some of it might come true, but in this case, only the last bit of dialogue was accurate.

THE ZAHAROFFS
OF TODAY

THE MAIN OFFICE OF THE International Armament Corporation was in a modern office building in the romantic city of Salzburg.

Received by a well-endowed secretary, I was led to a tastefully furnished office bearing the nameplate SAM CUMMINGS, PRESIDENT on its door.

However, there seemed to be a misunderstanding, because the only occupant of the room was a young American, obviously a college boy. I was greeted with a radiant smile and a friendly hello.

This would be the grandson or perhaps the youngest private secretary of the world's biggest weapons dealer, I thought.

Then a second man entered, shook hands with me, and said: "I'm Werner Glatt, vice president of Interarmco. I see you've already met the boss."

Completely bewildered, I stared first at Glatt, then at the other young man. *"You* are the president of Interarmco, the world's biggest weapons dealer?"

"Of course," was Sam Cummings's friendly reply, "but only for arms up to 40 millimeters. Our merchandise includes, of course, large calibers also, even airplanes, tanks, and warships. But these areas are mainly the territory of other big organizations. In the sale of rifles, machine guns, and the appropriate ammunition, however, our sales are by far the highest."

"We also have our own factories," said Vice President Glatt. He was not so tall as Cummings, wore his dark-blond hair in a crew cut, and appeared even more boyish than his president. "We are the owners of several armament plants in England and have a sizable interest in the Dutch subsidiary of Fairchild Engine and Airplane Corporation."

He handed me an illustrated catalog from which I learned that the Fairchild subsidiary was closely connected with Interarmco, and under the trade name Armalite* produced a late-model, fully automatic multipurpose assault gun capable of firing 700 shots per minute.

The title page of the catalog carried the slogan "Buy weapons from Interarmco!" There were many other interesting details, for example, that some old-established European armaments manufacturers were closely associated with Interarmco. Interarmco either acted as their general sales representatives or was the sole importer for these firms' products in certain territories. In many countries FN rifles from Belgium, Walther pistols from Ulm, quick-firing guns made by Hispano-Suiza, or automatic pistols from Munich's Erma-Werke could be bought only through Interarmco's local representatives.

While I was leafing through the brochure, the two young gentlemen spread out more pamphlets and statistics to emphasize Interarmco's importance and magnitude.

I learned that their organization did not confine its activities to the manufacture and sale of new weapons but that their principal business was buying and selling used arms and equipment.

Many countries, even entire continents, were again and again worked over by Interarmco's buyers, until the last rusty

---

* Editor's note: An Armalite line is also manufactured in the United States by Colt Firearms.

blunderbuss was dug up and in Interarmco's possession. The quantities of old weapons acquired in this way was staggering. In Western Europe and Scandinavia alone, eager Interarmco buyers had located and conveyed to Interarmco warehouses 20 million small arms of all types!

This part of Interarmco's activities could be considered praiseworthy, and even beneficial to peace; however, the disposition of these weapons changed the picture.

The millions of carbines, pistols, and machine guns bought by Interarmco for junk prices were by no means to be sold as scrap metal. They were sorted out, cleaned, repaired, and again offered on the market—for an adequate profit.

An old German Mauser carbine, left behind in Spain by Hitler's Condor Legion, discovered by Interarmco buyers and bought for $3.50, was back on the market two weeks later, cleaned and greased, for $27.95 plus freight for sale to any interested party. And there was no lack of buyers.

However, two conditions had to be met by Sam Cummings's customers: They had to be financially sound and in a position to pay cash. This was comparatively easy for most interested buyers because there is always money available for weapons.

The second condition raised considerable difficulties for some buyers: Interarmco's sales were restricted to those who enjoyed Washington's or, at least, the CIA's favor.

Sam Cummings, when a greenhorn of just twenty-five, surprised the old hands in the United States weapons business with an amazing transaction. He obtained a permit from Washington to export weapons from the United States to the president of Guatemala, Arkenz ("Red") Guzmán, hated by many big United States firms because of his leftist tendencies. Cummings bought some 10,000 Sten guns from United States Army stocks for 50¢ apiece, resold them without a qualm to Guzmán, for $4.00

apiece, plus shipping and insurance, net cash, with official documents.

This was Act I in an affair that would make Interarmco famous.

Act II started with an outcry by United States firms with interests in Guatemala who immediately felt threatened by Guzmán. In order to offset the damage, under the leadership of the United Fruit Company and the major oil companies, a syndicate was formed to negotiate with Cummings.

The first meeting produced a satisfactory agreement: Interarmco was to arm to the teeth Guatemala's neighbors also, selling them even more weapons than Guatemala to keep matters in balance.

Her neighbors, Honduras, Nicaragua, and El Salvador paid much higher prices than those Guzmán had been able to afford under great sacrifice. According to plan, Cummings then allowed further purchases by Guatemala but at still higher prices!

President Guzmán, who up to that time had been working out his small country's social problems without the aid of the Communist bloc, had no choice but to approach Moscow and Prague.

With this, he unwittingly triggered an internal uprising, what his neighbors had hoped for, and all parties were armed with American weapons supplied through Interarmco. Guzmán was finally overthrown and replaced by a military junta that enjoyed the favor of the United Fruit Company. Peace returned to Central America, and Sam Cummings made his first millions and secured a place in the international weapons market.

But this was only the beginning.

A few weeks later, the Government of Costa Rica was in need of arms. Washington did not want to interfere directly with the internal affairs of the Central American countries, but asked Cummings to satisfy Costa Rica's wishes. Thousands of crates of weapons were loaded on transport planes for quick dispatch. Sam Cummings's role as middleman was to buy the merchandise and sell it to Costa Rica's ambassador, for an appropriate profit, of course. The planes took off for Costa Rica, and its government relaxed. Thanks to Sam Cummings's intervention the danger of a *coup d'état* against American interests subsided.

With what I had just learned, I was not surprised when over a glass of lemonade Cummings revealed the names of some of his customers. Among those he recalled proudly were Jiménez, Perón, Batista, and Castro (at their meeting he was still friendly with the United States), but principally he remembered the Dominican Republic's "bloody Hector," ex-President Trujillo, who, to the relief of his subjects, is now dead. All those bloodstained hands had been shaken by Cummings during his transactions.

Trujillo earned the young Interarmco president's special regard. The dictator ordered unusual and precious weapons for his bodyguards—rifles with silver-plated barrels and gleaming bayonets; and he always paid promptly, a highly applauded virtue at Interarmco.

Supplying Latin American dictators with weapons constituted only the beginning of Interarmco's ascent. Soon, other, much more profitable, lines of business were explored, such as dealing in old weapons.

Interarmco's warehouses were filled with the remnants of war, and soon Cummings had more infantry weapons at his disposal than the entire British Army. He boasted that he was now in a position to outfit German, Russian, British, or American infantry divisions with their respective World War II weapons.

As satisfying as this fact might appear to him, I asked myself what use a private businessman would have for this enormous accumulation of arms.

My question was at least partly answered by Cummings himself: "We sell most of these weapons in the United States," he told me. "We have our own mail-order organization there from which every possible weapon can be bought COD, and you have no idea how many Americans like to have a war trophy to decorate their walls or gardens!"

Right. I had no idea, but looking at the balance sheet of the United States mail-order house convinced me that there had to be hundreds of thousands. But the demand at home was not enough to justify Interarmco's stocks.

Cummings was unwilling to name his customer for used weapons outside the United States.

Nor would Glatt—who looked even more like an American than Cummings but who was German—reveal any details about such customers. His statements were vague and generalized.

"Under no circumstances do we sell without a license!" he emphasized over and over.

Uneasy and not quite satisfied, I left and drove back to Munich.

During a stroll through this city one evening, I met my old friend Hans Joachim Seidenschnur.

Though I thought it could not be possible, he appeared even more elegant than before. "Everything is going well!" he assured me after the first whiskey. "I live in Munich now. I moved here from Bonn."

"What happened to the Liaison Office of Belgian Armaments Manufacturers?" I inquired. "Have they moved, too?"

"I am through with them!" said Seidenschnur contemptuously. "These little transactions of a few tons of TNT or a few thousand carbines are finally over!"

"You did not change your occupation?" I asked in amazement.

Seidenschnur had advanced in his career; but his métier remained unchanged. "I now represent the world's biggest weapons dealer," he said in a confident voice, loud enough for everybody to hear.

I was surprised. Could there be another giant in the weapons trade?

But Seidenschnur was not the man to leave the press in ignorance. He pulled out a small case made from genuine crocodile skin, opened it painstakingly, and handed me his business card:

Hans Joachim Seidenschnur
Legal Adviser
Representative of International Armament Corporation

"Now you are surprised, aren't you?" he said.

I was.

"In a few days we are going to establish a subsidiary company here in Munich, the 'German Interarmco,' and the manager will be Hans Joachim Seidenschnur," he continued. "Then the way is free, and work can start."

"What are your plans?" I inquired.

"We will start some clean-up action here," explained Puchert's ex-partner. "We will put a stop to those who discredit our trade with their criminal practices, their inferior merchandise, and ridiculous prices."

"And how are you going to do this?" I asked, but Seidenschnur was not revealing his plans for ridding the German arms market of undesirable elements.

Instead he detailed his ideas of how to manage the German branch of Interarmco.

"We will buy everything," he announced, "clear out all depots that now apply pressure on the market, clear out the old Germany Army surplus in arsenals in the Balkans and in hiding places all over West Germany. We will buy all these weapons and pay hard cash, you understand?"

I understood.

"And when we have all the used weapons that are still around, concentrated in one place, we will start to sell. Negotiations have begun, but we will take our time. We can wait."

"And with whom are you negotiating?" I inquired.

"First with the Algerians. We will make them an offer better than any they have received. We will supply their needs on credit, and will expect payment only after Algeria has gained independence, probably in the form of surplus weapons, which they should have left over in large quantities in Africa."

I nodded agreeably, hoping that Seidenschnur would divulge more of his ideas.

"I have made contact with the natives in Angola," he continued. "Very soon a new market will open up there, when the rebellion against the Portuguese begins."

"But doesn't your organization supply the white settlers in Angola and elsewhere in Africa?" I asked in amazement.

Seidenschnur made a grandiose gesture.

"The world is wide," he said; "we must help everybody to the best of our abilities. Of course, we do not supply the white settlers and colored natives through the same department. The German branch of Interarmco will act as a neutral intermediary, but only on paper, of course. The merchandise itself comes from the same depot."

He revealed many more interesting details. But the most amazing was still to come:

"I am thinking of a 'triangular deal,'" said Seidenschnur before we parted. "The German branch of Interarmco buys old German Army carbines in Hungary and Bulgaria, paying in hard currency that these countries need so badly, and sells them to the East German People's Army. Payment is made in Zeiss binoculars and telescopic sights. Negotiations in East Berlin are forthcoming."

This was enough for me.

I decided to pay Cummings a second visit in Salzburg. I went there the following week, but he had gone, so I was received by Glatt, though he, too, was preparing to leave.

"We're moving," he said. "We've transferred our main office to Monte Carlo. Come and visit us if you should happen to be around!" He then gave me an ashtray decorated with the Salzburg coat of arms and the inscription INTERARMCO in gold.

I was quite moved, and promised to see them soon in Monte Carlo.

I kept my word. Ten days later I pressed the bell at the entrance to an ultramodern apartment house in the center of Monte Carlo. The nameplate read:

Interarmco Industrial Group
Office of the President

Cummings opened the door. He was dressed in an open-necked sportshirt and colorful beach shorts.

"How nice of you to come to see us," he said when he opened the door. He carried a rifle in one hand; in the other he held a disassembled oily lock and a rag. "Well," I said, "are you doing your own maintenance now?"

He laughed.

"That would be quite a job!" he said. "At present we have 850,000 such rifles in our American depots alone. I'm taking care only of my private collection, but the main part of it is in London, in Churchill House, which is owned by the British Interarmco. It's a unique collection—better than the one in the British Museum. You should really go and see it!"

I admitted that my interest in weapons was more, so to speak, of a political nature.

But he objected.

"Politics," he said, "is not for businessmen."

"But it provides your living," I replied. "Without the tensions in the world and the Cold War, you would be out of business!"

He did not agree.

"Of course, the Cold War is good for our business," he said, "but weapons become obsolete fast, political tension or not. They're always in demand: The big countries replace yesterday's weapons with today's; the small countries replace the weapons of the day before yesterday's with yesterday's."

"And what happens to the weapons from two days before yesterday?" I asked further.

Cummings smiled. "They become souvenirs or . . ." He hesitated.

I finished the sentence for him: ". . . such weapons become expensive when sold to people who are not yet in power, but want to fight for it!"

"Of course," he said, "that happens. It's like that in politics."

"Didn't you say that you are not influenced by politics?" I reminded him politely.

The successor:
college boy Sam Cummings, boss
of Interarmco.

Photo: Ottfried Schmidt, Munich

Next to the top in the international weapons business:
Ernst Wilhelm Glatt, Interarmco Vice President.

Photo: Petra Engelmann, Hamburg

Cummings nodded.

"That's the way it is," he said. "For me, dealing in weapons is only business, strictly business. And Interarmco is now so big and powerful that we can—and must—do without smuggling, black-market business, rebellious natives, and shifty characters."

I remembered Seidenschnur and the exquisite stationery with the gold-embossed motto ESSE QUAM VIDERI—"To Be Rather Than to Seem."

I couldn't think of a more appropriate motto for Interarmco!

That evening, sitting on a rocky terrace above Monaco and looking down at the colored lights of the Casino and the Hôtel de Paris, I thought of the old Zaharoff who had died there, and of the "new Zaharoff" who lived just around the corner. When I looked out over the Mediterranean, I thought of the French, German, Arab, and Kabyle divisions dying in North Africa by carbines, machine guns, and mortars from Interarmco's warehouses. I remembered a much better motto for Interarmco, one Sam Cummings had mentioned and that could be engraved not only on stationery but on every pistol and hand grenade—"Only business, strictly business."

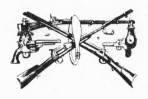

BUSINESS, BUSINESS
ABOVE ALL

THE EVENTS IN THE PREVIOUS CHAPTERS occurred a few years ago.

Since my meeting with Sam Cummings, I focused my investigation on the users of arms.

In the rugged valleys of the Algerian Aurès, on the eastern slopes of the Atlas Mountains, and on long trips over the paths through the Sahara Desert, I saw men handling Finnish mortars, old German 2cm antiaircraft guns, and new Italian Beretta pistols.

In Oran I watched young German adventurers, wearing the uniform of the French Foreign Legion, shooting at French police officers with German MG42 machine guns they had captured from the Algerians.

In Guinea, where the borders of about six new and old countries meet over swamp holes and fieldstones, I inspected crates containing hand grenades, flamethrowers, and machine-gun parts, whose origin and purpose were hotly contested by representatives of the different hostile groups in this area. However, I discovered the real origin of these weapons. Half were sold by respectable merchants from Cologne and Dortmund to emissaries from Communist China, and the profits immediately deposited in the Liechtenstein bank. The other half came from a German firm, MEREX, which will be discussed later.

In Cuba I watched in awe the invasion of the Bay of Pigs and its ensuing slaughter with weapons bought from Interarmco —by both sides. Cuba's defenders attacked with Russian tanks, carried NATO rifles of the FN type, and Armalite assault guns with rocket-launching attachments, part of an Interarmco shipment to Castro at a time the bearded rebel was thought to be a reliable friend of the United States.

The invasion force, equipped and sent into a hopeless battle by the CIA, were also armed with weapons from Interarmco; in fact, Cummings sold a part of them to "Red" Guzmán's neighbors.

Compared with all this, those sales by Puchert, Seidenschnur, Lie, Springer, Beissner, Schlüter, Petersen. and the countess appear trifling.

But then why should I be more concerned with these small-time merchants than with Cummings and his Communist colleagues and their billion-dollar deals? Because the minor league is more interesting. Not even the tycoons in the business could operate without the cooperation of these minor merchants.

Many of the characters the reader has met in this book have been or are now working for Interarmco or Omnipol— those who are still living and who are not in prison.

Hans Joachim Seidenschnur was one of those who was sent to prison. I had last seen Seidenschnur in Munich, where he had just been appointed the German representative of the International Armament Corporation. Shortly after our meeting, the German Interarmco GmbH had been established in an exclusive hotel between Munich and Salzburg, but the firm's life was to be of short duration. When Glatt and Cummings discovered that their manager's expenses were out of proportion with actual sales, Seidenschnur decided to bring his extravagant standards more in line with those of a middle-class citizen.

Befitting someone ready to begin a new chapter in his

life, he performed a good deed: He married the mother of his child. But he did much more than merely bestow his name. The little girl had an eye deficiency, and Seidenschnur made a genuine and touching effort to have this corrected. He approached a famous surgeon. After all, Seidenschnur was the representative of a huge American corporation, and should have only the best. The surgeon was very impressed. The operation was a success. The little girl was pampered and spoiled as never before. And the respect a father gets for his efforts to have the finest surgeon perform an operation on his daughter should be no less simply because he never paid the medical and hospital bills.

However, it was not the doctor who finally took Seidenschnur to court, but Interarmco. In an incredibly short time, the funds for their German subsidiary were exhausted, and Seidenschnur's pending business appeared to hold no prospects of compensation.

It was not surprising, therefore, that his employers in Monte Carlo terminated his employment and audited his books. There was a trial and he went to jail.

I obtained a visitor's pass from the district attorney's office in Munich, and on a dreary, rainy day in the fall I traveled to the Chiemsee, one of the famous Bavarian lakes, where the notorious Bernau Prison provided temporary lodgings for my friend.

I expected he would be bent with grief, his complexion turned to a pale-gray, hollow-cheeked, his back sore from working in the nearby peat bog. . . .

A surly guard opened the door and explained gruffly that I had come at the wrong time. He did not even care to inspect my pass, but when I told him whom I came to see, he became friendly and almost servile.

"Oh, you want to see Herr Seidenschnur; that is different, of course."

I was led to a bare visitors' room, and then the guard held the door open for a gentleman I at first thought to be the warden. He was somewhat dashing, dressed in lounging clothes, suitable for a director of a fashionable winter resort—suntanned, looking well rested and relaxed.

"I am so glad to see you," said Seidenschnur, "but I can spend only about fifteen minutes with you because I am right in the middle of a very important and confidential transaction." He glanced in the direction of the guard, who listened respectfully and, when asked, confirmed this statement with a meaningful nod. Then Seidenschnur turned again to me and said, like a bank president disturbed by a trivial matter on a Sunday morning, "Now then, what can I do for you?"

Several months later I met Seidenschnur again, this time in the lobby of the Bayerische Hof, a luxury hotel in Munich. As usual, he looked exceedingly well, and appeared in a hurry.

"I will be traveling to China tomorrow," he said, and when I asked whom he would represent there, he mentioned a dozen firms of excellent reputation. This proved to be true when I checked him out later. Three well-known organizations apparently had hired him when he was an inmate of Bernau, and they must have met him at the prison gate. Only weeks after his release, he was again on top—on board a luxury liner sailing to the Far East, carrying in his morocco leather case offers of all kinds, recommendations to high-ranking Communist officials, and traveler's checks for five-digit amounts.

The result of his confidential work at Bernau was the dispatch to Iran of large crates, marked with the shipper's name, "MEREX." The crates contained 3,000 machine guns, caliber .30, with 30 million rounds of ammunition, and a further 25 million rounds of ammunition of other calibers.

As part of this enormous transaction, there were 90 United States F86 Saber jets from surplus stock of the German Federal Army. They were bought by MEREX officially for Iran (unofficially for Pakistan), and pilots of the German Air Force ferried them to Iran.

Shortly after this, MEREX bought some Seahawk jet fighters. The seller, the Bonn Defense Ministry, had them flown to Italy, but it appeared they were unaware of the fact that the Seahawks would travel on to India. These tactics were employed to bypass an international embargo on war matériel to Pakistan and India, who were fighting over Kashmir.

Other business—always involving surplus matériel from the German Federal Army—provided arms for Jordan, Saudi Arabia, and the United Arab Republic, which were used against Israel. The Israelis procured their weapons from other sources.

There now remains the question of the connection between MEREX and Seidenschnur. A satisfactory answer is not easy to give, not for its difficulty but because of certain paragraphs contained in the German Penal Code.

Why? Well, let us assume, hypothetically, that an Intelligence agent had interrogated Seidenschnur in prison and was, at the same time, on a friendly basis with MEREX. This could explain a great deal, but it would also be an official secret.

Of course, this was not true, because the Bonn Government emphatically denied any knowledge of these transactions with Pakistan and India, and made it quite clear that they disapproved of such practices. During this period Ludwig Erhard was Chancellor, and Ludger Westrick was Secretary of State (and responsible for the Intelligence agency). Westrick was in a good position to know whether MEREX had been involved in illegal transactions—even if he had not been informed through Intelligence—because his son Fritz was then second in command of MEREX and the right hand to the director, Gerhard Mertins.

Mertins, a former major in Hermann Goering's paratroop division, held the *Ritterkreuz*, then Germany's Order of Merit, and had after World War II been a car salesman in Egypt before joining MEREX.

The aforementioned transaction with Pakistan (via Iran) brought MEREX a profit of approximately $4,000,000. Hence, Mertins could afford to buy a château in La Tour de Peilz on Lake Geneva; a country mansion in Villars-sur-Ollon; a beauti-

ful house on the Rhine near Bonn; a luxury yacht; and a fleet
of impressive limousines and sports cars.

But where there is prosperity, there is envy.

Early in 1967, a press campaign against Mertins and
MEREX commenced, mainly in Switzerland. A leading magazine published a detailed report with alarming information,
demanding the expulsion of Mertins from Switzerland. Naturally, I was interested in the material and its source. Provided
with the files on the case by a friendly colleague, I was going
through them when a business card slipped out, bearing the
notation:

For your convenience
presented by
International Armament Corporation
Office of the President

At the time, Sam Cummings was having his own troubles. He
was giving testimony to a Congressional Subcommittee in the
United States, information he would have liked to have kept
to himself.

It would be naïve to assume that the weapons business has
suffered a blow because of press campaigns, investigations,
trials, and convictions. German courts in Hamburg, Kiel, and
Munich have convicted a number of international arms merchants; in other countries there were actions of moral condem-
nation; and still the lucrative business with death continues.
While this is being written, chartered planes land on the runways
of African airports in Kano and Lagos, unloading arms and
ammunition for the battle over Biafra, and return for another
cargo. And tomorrow they will unload their deadly wares at
another place: perhaps Latin America, the Balkans, or the
Middle East.

These merchants are unconcerned about who their customers are and how their merchandise is used. They are far more concerned with competition from the many small adventurers who create pressure on the market. These amateurs adversely affect whatever respectability the trade has achieved, and many of them subsequently end in court.

But court actions involving illegal weapons transactions are usually brief and inadequate, with minimal influence on jury verdicts. This may hurt the feelings of some of the accused, because even weapons dealers have their professional pride, particularly in a society where it is of no significance how a man earns his living but rather how much he earns.

I hope I have compensated the merchants for their suffering by writing this report. Perhaps by portraying them as they really are, they will become examples worthy of emulation, along with pop singers, ex-royalty, striptease dancers, professional athletes, or investment bankers, inspiring new commercials, such as "Successful weapons dealers drink XY whiskey," or *"If* they live, they live comfortably with ZZZ cigarettes."

To those readers who are repulsed by the weapons merchants' activities, and who consider Captain Morris, Otto the Strange One, Little Napoléon, the countess, slick Glatt, and jovial Seidenschnur not at all charming, and would encourage a public outcry to halt the illegal sale of arms, I can assure them of this: The business will go on just as before; the men and women described on these pages will remain faithful to their trade (those who have not been eliminated), including the countess with her new husband, a banker who is a member of the boards of directors of well-known corporations in Düsseldorf, Essen, and other major centers in the Ruhr area.

Every society is what its people make it.

Postscript

ARMS MERCHANT
TO THE WORLD

by Sanche de Gramont*

SAMUEL CUMMINGS IS THE LARGEST PRIVATE ARMS DEALER
in the world. He concedes that selling guns is different from
selling encyclopedias or Fuller brushes. The primary function
of a gun is to kill. When the National Rifle Association tells
us that there are proportionately far more traffic deaths than
gunshot deaths per year in the United States, so that if you
are going to outlaw the free sale of guns you might as well outlaw the free sale of cars, the obvious reply is that, unless the
people in Detroit are more malevolent than anyone thinks,
homicide is not the primary function of the automobile. But
does a salesman have moral control over his product? Is it the
pharmacist's fault if the little old lady with the flowered hat
spikes her husband's breakfast cereal with sulfuric acid? Are
distillers responsible for drunks? Are gun dealers to blame for
wars, murders, and hunting accidents?

And yet guns are different because they are by definition
lethal and because the armaments business has a tarnished past.
Thus, according to publications like *Der Spiegel, Pravda,* and the

Journal de Genève, Sam Cummings has inherited the mantle of the sinister Sir Basil Zaharoff (1850–1936), the arms dealer for whom the terms "peddler of death" and "devil's smithy" were coined.

Aside from the fact that both men chose Monte Carlo as their place of residence, there is not much resemblance between the bearded, Svengali-like Zaharoff and Cummings, the proto-type of the back slapper, who is about as sinister as Santa Claus and likes nothing better than to make sardonic jokes about the peculiarities of his profession. Today, Cummings points out, since 99 percent of the world's armaments are sold by govern-ments, private merchants are no longer the manipulators of policy, but merely its agents. The sordid mercantilism and political intrigues of Zaharoff, Krupp, Vickers, and the other pre–World War I munitions giants no longer are characteristic of the private-arms field.

Cummings seems rather to have inherited what might be called the Rhett Butler mentality. As the dashing but pragmatic Civil War blockade runner put it: "What most people don't seem to realize is that there is just as much money to be made out of the wreckage of a civilization as from the upbuilding of one." Rhett Butler sold Confederate cotton to England and brought back guns for the rebels, disclaiming patriotic involve-ment. His philosophy was free enterprise, right or wrong, and he insisted that "blockading is a business with me and I'm making money out of it. When I stop making money out of it, I'll quit."

In the same manner, although his business is strictly legal, weapons have made the forty-year-old Cummings a millionaire, and he is ready to sell anything from a hunting knife to a jet fighter to any nation able to afford it. Half of his worldwide business consists of selling light arms on the American and Commonwealth markets. The other half involves acting as broker for international arms deals. He benefits from conflagra-tions, for either the belligerents are fighting with his weapons, or one side will eventually have surplus armament to dispose of.

He is currently negotiating with the Israeli Government to purchase Soviet light arms captured in the six-day war. Cummings sees no harm in profiting from what he calls "our era's treadmill to oblivion." He believes that "arms are the symbol of man's folly throughout the ages. That's what civilization was, is, and always will be: 'Open up! Let 'em have it!' That's why this is the only business that should last forever."

"I should laugh diabolically and put on my Dr. Faustus mask," Cummings said when I asked him about the merchant-of-death image. "But I simply point to our license file—we do less than 1 percent of the United States Government's business and we have Government approval of every deal."

Since 1957, the Pentagon has been conducting arms sales through an innocuous-sounding agency known as International Logistics Negotiations, which supplies its NATO partners and twenty-four other countries with a complete range of weapons. The Government's three main reasons for taking a major share of the armaments market seem to be: To offset the balance-of-payments deficit created by United States military expenditures abroad; to boost employment at home and profits for American industries; and the belief that it is healthier for allies who can afford it to pay for their own defense.

Henry J. Kuss, Jr., the Deputy Assistant Secretary of Defense in charge of arms sales, proudly explains American leadership in the arms field by saying that "no other nation can touch us in overall technological know-how, quality, price, delivery time, follow-up logistical support and credit terms." From $600 million in fiscal 1961, Mr. Kuss and his twenty-one-man sales force increased weapons sales to $1.93 billion in fiscal 1966.

Cummings declines to qualify his annual sales figures in more specific terms than "in eight figures" and "under $100 million." He is able to compete with the United States Government because he cuts prices and, as he says, "a small company can give quick, efficient service." For instance, the Government is still selling World War II Browning .50-caliber machine guns at $750 each, the cost of manufacture. Cummings, who buys

Brownings as surplus from governments stocking more modern equipment, reconditions them and sells them at $265. "We can give these savings right through the weapons spectrum," he says. "For instance, we are offering United States tanks at a far lower cost than the Government."

He owns more than 100,000 square feet of warehouses on the banks of the Potomac in Alexandria, Virginia, which are stocked with 50,000 pistols, 10,000 machine guns, 600,000 rifles, and 100 million cartridges. There are 300,000 more assorted weapons neatly stacked in his London warehouses. He has 200 employees, 17 affiliates and subsidiaries, and agents around the world who keep him informed about possible arms deals. Many of these are retired generals or high civil servants with entrees to their governments; until recently his agent in Indonesia was President Sukarno's cousin.

Cummings works out of a fourteen-room apartment in Monaco, ten rooms of which serve as the residence for himself, his blonde, Swiss-born wife Irma, and his five-year-old towheaded twin daughters. His office is decorated with an eighteenth-century English two-pounder, a sixteenth-century German suit of armor, a large map of the world (courtesy of the United States Army map service) and photographs of artillery being unloaded from boat decks in a Latin American harbor onto rail cars, with smiling generals in the background.

Cummings prohibits the use of Telex between his many branches, for he says he would "just be broadcasting my moves to the competition." He discourages interoffice telephone calls, and uses a number code in his business correspondence to designate countries and types of armament. His coded files contain the military secrets of rival nations, so that he has to maintain James Bond–like security.

Every foreign sale Cummings makes depends on licensing from the State Department or, if Commonwealth countries are involved, the British War Office. "In a strict legal sense there's nothing they could do if I went ahead without their OK," he says, "but practically it would be extremely unwise. I have $10 million worth of installations in the United States and I depend on the goodwill of the Government. Any manufacturer of whiskey could sell bootleg to his chums after hours, but would it really pay Calvert to do that?

"Our biggest headache is getting policy from the State Department. I was recently approached by a Latin American country for the delivery of 50 light American M-41 tanks. These are good tanks which NATO considers obsolescent, so that NATO nations want to unload them. I made a detailed proposition to the Minister of Defense of that country, subject to United States approval. I have the NATO power's approval for the sale. But at State they've been stalling since June.

"Meanwhile, the same country has received a proposal from France, which offers facilities to assemble their new light tank, the AMX-30, in the country itself, and offers long-term, low-interest financing. If I don't close the deal by the end of the month I'll lose by default. The chance to supply a standard United States item to a Latin American country that receives United States aid will be lost to France—the United States aid will be helping the French economy."

To sell his staple—light arms—Cummings is on the road eight months a year. As a result, Spanish *carabinieri,* Yugoslav border police, Finnish army patrols, and many other armed forces are carrying rifles sold by his company, Interarmco, or one of its affiliates.

Cummings is the sole private agent for the products of the Dutch, Swedish, and Finnish national arms factories, and has an open-end agreement with Colt to sell its lightweight, rapid-fire Armalite rifle, the latest model of which the Marines are using in Vietnam. Colt, of course, favors its own retailers, but Cummings is able to find many markets for the Armalite thanks to his resourceful salesmanship.

He travels with an Armalite M14 or M16 neatly disassembled in a flat Fiberglas case lined with foam rubber, and thus far has had no trouble at customs. He also carries a magnet to test the quality of cartridge cases and a micrometer to measure the wear on gun bores of surplus weapons he might consider as trade-ins for new guns.

Arriving in a foreign capital, he calls up the Minister of Defense and says: "I'm here to demonstrate the best rifle in the world." If an important sale is involved, he may present the chief of state with a gold-plated pistol or some other memento. The prospective customers "are always interested," he says, "because everybody likes fireworks. I use tracer bullets. If you can see it, you believe it. I assemble the rifle to show how easy it is. I fire at normal targets at different ranges. I'm a pretty good shot. I get plenty of practice. Then for the grand finale I fill a few bean cans full of petrol—did you ever see a tracer bullet hit a bean can full of petrol? It's better than a John Wayne movie. This little demonstration never fails to elicit delightful Oh's and Ah's. I saddle up and ride into the sunset, leaving the firing range a smoldering ruin."

At a Senate hearing a few months ago, Cummings gave his candid opinion of the Armalite rifle, which he has successfully sold from Cuba to Kenya, and which, as the M16, has been the subject of intense controversy concerning its performance in Vietnam. The testimony went this way:

CUMMINGS: "I am not personally an enthusiast of it."

SYMINGTON: "In South Vietnam they are enthusiastic because of the weight."

CUMMINGS: "The World War II carbine was a useless weapon. It was light. Everybody loved it because it was light, but it was a dog."

SYMINGTON: "Why was it a dog?"

CUMMINGS: "Ballistically, you can have a hatful of cartridges in your stomach and still live long enough to blast the man who fired at you. It is as simple as that."

At this point, the anonymous recorder of the hearings, bent in concentration over his Stenotype machine, jumped up and said: "He's right; he's right. I was in the Battle of the Bulge and I shot a German six times with a carbine and he was still able to shoot me."

His remarks went unrecorded, as did Cummings's private opinion that "if I was a Marine in Vietnam and was given one of those new Armalites, I'd throw it away and say I'd lost it and try to get one of the Russian rifles off a dead V.C. They're the best."

Cummings has no qualms about supplying both sides in a conflict. "Any supplier of basic commodities sells to both sides," he says. "Coca-Cola sells to both Arabs and Israelis." When you are selling guns, however, the results can be embarrassing. Cuba's Fulgencio Batista had been one of Cummings's regular customers. When Fidel Castro overthrew him in 1959, Cummings kept supplying the new regime with Armalite rifles until the State Department stopped licensing weapons sales to Cuba.

Some time later, Cummings was in the Dominican Republic demonstrating the Armalite to Trujillo. A group of Cuban-based guerrillas had just landed at Puerto Plata. General Kovacs, Trujillo's Hungarian-born military adviser, was examining a captured Cuban rifle on his desk when Cummings came in with Trujillo.

One word led to another, and Cummings finally had to admit that it was he who had sold the captured rifle to Castro. "You know I wouldn't tell him to use it against you," Cummings blandly told Trujillo.

Cummings is also fully conscious that he sells arms to underdeveloped countries which are diverting hard currency from social reforms to buy them, and whose leaders are exponents of Goering's adage that "guns will make us powerful; butter will only make us fat."

"They think they must have the weapons to parade down the main boulevard on Independence Day," Cummings says, "and make the people think they are safer than they are as they shout, *'Viva la libertad,'* when what they should be shouting is,

'*Adios libertad.*' It's the same whether it's a people's democracy
or an emerging nation. These are the empty passwords of our
times. Emerging from what? The only word I know in Russian is
skoro—'soon.' How many times I have seen the obedient masses
marching onward toward the promise of *skoro*.

"In the final analysis, the morality of armaments boils down
to who makes the sale. I have to make them buy my model. The
East bloc salesman comes to Egypt, slaps the admiral on the
back, and presents him with a battleship he can't sail on a sea
he doesn't own near a coast he can't approach."

Since Cummings has been in the arms business, he has noticed
some progress, not in international morality, but in reducing
international hypocrisy. "The sales pitch of arms dealers," he
says, "used to stress offensives: 'If you buy these new machine
guns you can blow those guys on the other side of the hill into
the Stone Age.' This isn't considered polite any more. You need
a defensive pitch: 'Unless you obtain this type of weapon you
won't have fire superiority in case of aggression. You won't even
make it out of your foxhole!' " Cummings eschews the expression
"A bigger bang for a buck."

Even with the defensive approach, Cummings is a con-
vincing enough salesman to have, on one occasion, badly
frightened a Central American dictator (name withheld because
he is still a Cummings client). "I'm well protected," the dictator
had told Cummings; "I have all I need."

"It's common knowledge that each morning you sit in front
of the same picture window in your national palace," replied
Cummings ominously. "All I need is a piston-engine plane
armed with eight 50mm machine guns. I'd come in low and
blast you through the window.

"Another thing—I wasn't even frisked when I came in here.
How do you know I can't send you to kingdom come with what
I've got in this attaché case?" Cummings reached for the case,
but a nervous bodyguard intercepted him at gunpoint. "You

know what the sea captain in *The Bridge of San Luis Rey* said,"
comments Cummings, " 'all so fake, Esteban.' "

A lifetime of studying and selling weapons has made Cummings
skeptical about human progress, which he tends to see in terms
of the era B.G. and A.G.—before and after gunpowder. He was
raised on Philadelphia's Main Line. His stockbroker father was
wiped out on Black Friday and became the manager of an
electrical supply store. He died when Sam was eight, and his
widow went into real estate so that she could send her son to the
exclusive Episcopal Academy there. Cummings later adopted the
school motto, *Esse Quam Videri* ("To Be Rather Than to
Seem"), for his company.

He became what he calls "a gun nut" at the age of five when
an American Legion post gave him a rusted World War I Maxim
machine gun, which he learned to assemble. He started a gun
collection, and by the time he was in his late teens he knew as
much about light arms as a master armorer.

He was drafted in 1945, and at close-order drill on the first
day of basic training he handled his rifle with such professional
ease that the sergeant, his face one inch from Cummings's
roared: "You've been in the Army before!"

Cummings missed the shooting war, but in 1948, with the
fervor of a Renaissance art scholar on his first visit to Tuscan
museums, he toured Europe to see the battle sites. In Nor-
mandy's Falaise Gap, in the Ardennes and in Western Germany,
Cummings saw fields that looked as though they had been
planted with tanks and heavy artillery. It was like finding pirate
treasure. "The cartridge belts were still on the machine guns," he
recalls. "The tanks had that new-car smell. All they needed was
a battery recharge to start 'em up and reconquer France."

He was distraught at the sight of this fine material going to
waste. "In Scandinavia, it was a tragedy," he says. "They took
all the German arms and dumped them into the sea."

Following his grand tour, Cummings was graduated from

George Washington University and served briefly as a clerk in the CIA, during the Korean war. He was put to work identifying North Korean weapons from photographs. Not unexpectedly, they were Russian. But the vision of arms-strewn European fields still haunted him, and he joined a small West Coast arms firm on a salary-plus-commission basis. Within two years, he had saved $25,000 to start his own business.

His first innovation was the purchase of large quantities of surplus light arms in Europe to sell on the American market. Cummings knew that the basis for every fine bolt-action sporting rifle is the German Mauser. He also knew that several European countries were overstocked with Mausers. They were the wrong caliber for NATO standardization, and cost money to maintain and store. They even cost money to throw away. Finally, Cummings had faith in the United States gun market. He estimates that there are 50 million armed American civilians, including 24 million registered hunters, many millions of unregistered hunters, collectors, veterans, and other types of gun nuts.

"Let's face it," he says, "the gun made this country. It's the frontier tradition, the musket over the fireplace, the man at the end of the Concord bridge. The gun's part of the language —'Keep your powder dry,' 'Lock, stock, and barrel,' 'Flash in the pan.' I used to visit local gunshops at the start of the hunting season on Saturday morning and watch one of these guys come in. He'd pick a Mauser out of the rack, put down a $20 bill, and his eyes would sort of glaze over, and you could see him thinking: 'Let 'em come, I'm ready!' "

Cummings bought out the entire stock of surplus light arms from several European countries, including hundreds of thousands of what he calls "arsenal-fresh Mausers, with Hitler's fingerprints still on them." He sometimes got them for as low as 10 percent of cost, which allowed him to offer substantial bargains on the American market. He also did the rounds of Washington's military attachés to ferret out unwanted surplus.

Gradually Cummings built up his domestic market to the point where he now sells 250,000 firearms a year in the United

States and 80,000 more in the Commonwealth. He bought out two famous English gunmakers, Grant and Lang and E. J. Churchill, and has increased production while maintaining their line of handmade shotguns that sell for $2,000 each. He is the only non-English member of a tight-knit *confrérie* called The Worshipful Company of Gunmakers, which confers obscure privileges, such as the right to ride in the Thames barge procession on Coronation Day.

In Finland, Cummings bought all the leftover weapons from the Russo-Finnish winter war, ranging from captured Cossack sabers to 20mm Finnish antitank guns, too light to pierce Russian armor. The Finns had fired them at the vision slits of Russian bunkers in Karelia.

Cummings is amused at the uses customers have found for the antitank guns. Some were sold to laboratories testing armor plate. Others went to a whale cooperative in Alaska, located near a spot where the whales come too close to shore for their own good. Cummings throws back his head and roars with laughter at the thought: "When the whale yawns, he swallows that red-hot slug—Gulp!"

An Arizona dentist who bought an antitank gun to shoot rabbits, reported: "I don't hit many, but when I do—Oh, man!"

Anti-Castro raiders used the Finnish 20mm to shoot up fuel dumps near Havana. Ignoring the fact that the weapon does not fire explosive shells, they managed only to spring a few leaks in the storage tanks.

Retailers who carry the antitank guns ran humorous ads in the National Rifle Association magazine, *The Rifleman:* "Always try for an eye-shot at the charging rhinoceros."

About this time Cummings also began to go after the big orders. In 1956 he sold 26 Swedish Vampire jets to Trujillo for $3.5 million. His biggest single deal, $20 million worth of arms, involved three countries and took a year and a half to negotiate.

Always wary of the competition, Cummings does not like to go into the details of his important brokerage deals. However, he does puncture the notion that arms dealers make huge profits.

His own average profit margin, he says, ranges from 9 percent to 12 percent. On one recent deal he obtained a supply of new Belgian rifles from West Germany. They cost $125 apiece at the factory, but he bought them as surplus for $35 each. It costs $7 per rifle for overhauling, and he sells them at $50 for a gross profit of nearly 20 percent.

Cummings is disdainful of the United States Government arms salesmen who are able to conclude much more important deals with a single telephone call. "Kuss doesn't know what a commercial operation is," he says. "He has the whole Department of Defense behind him. All he has to do is answer the phone."

The arms race between the two great power blocs helps Cummings thrive, for it makes perfectly good NATO weapons obsolete the moment Russian matériel improves. In 1970, Cummings is expecting 4,000 M47 United States tanks to come up for sale in NATO countries. "It's first-class goods," he says, "never used except on short maneuvers. It's just what the rest of the world doesn't need but must have for their own useless maneuvers."

At a hearing last April 13, Cummings tried to convey some of the absurdities of the arms business to senators on the Subcommittee on Near Eastern and South Asian Affairs, chaired by Senator Stuart Symington. The mere fact that the United States tries to match Soviet arms deliveries, Cummings said, "will encourage the Soviet Union to put its thumb on the scales and throw it out of kilter. Look at Afghanistan. . . . We give the Afghans some airfields and a beautiful highway, and the Russians rush in with an armored division, and then we give them, I think, some aircraft, and it goes on and on. A case of 'Can you top this!' There is no end to it."

The senators were particularly concerned about 90 United States F86 jet fighters West Germany had sold to Iran, which

was acting as a clearinghouse for Pakistan. A NATO embargo
on weapons sales to either India or Pakistan had been circum-
vented, thanks to the device of using Iran as a cover. The planes
had been sold through a private German broker, but had been
flown to Iran by *Luftwaffe* pilots in civilian clothes. The so-
called end-use agreement, by which the United States exercises
a veto on the resale of its military equipment, had been disre-
garded.

The senators, who had just heard details of this questionable transaction for the first time, were dismayed to learn from
Cummings that it was common knowledge in European government and military circles. "There are wonderful regulations and
pronouncements of policy," said Cummings, "but the plainest
print cannot be read through a gold eagle."

"Well," said Senator Symington, "that is quite an observation."

Cummings sees the arms business as a series of hopeless
contradictions. The West Germans are glutted with arms they
don't need, and Chancellor Kiesinger is urged to buy more
weapons each time he comes to Washington. And the senators
are surprised because the Germans try to unload some of their
excess hardware on the Pakistanis. The Soviet Union, to take
another example. is the champion of emerging nations but sells
arms to South Africa. The United States, probably the most
vocal nation in the world when it comes to disarmament, is also
the world's biggest salesman of modern weapons. As a man
whose business depends on such anomalies, Cummings is fond
of commenting on the futility of life, and adds: "Fortunately, as
the old sea captain said, 'It's not for long, Esteban.' "

On the subject of disarmament, Cummings believes with
Plato that "only the dead have known the end of war."

"Disarmament," Cummings says, "will never happen." One
of the few disarmament goals ever achieved—the banning of the
dumdum bullet—came about, he argues, because of a develop-
ment in weaponry: New high-velocity rifles could not take a
soft-nosed bullet.

He is less sanguine about proposed laws to curtail the sale and distribution of firearms in the United States, which would cut into his domestic market, and he echoes the standard arguments of the National Rifle Association. The Dodd bill, which would prohibit the mail-order purchase of light arms, "penalizes the honest sportsman and the law-abiding collector. The misuse of weapons should be penalized, rather than have a law which prevents John Jones, deer hunter in upper Nebraska, from carrying cartridges in his car across the state line."

At the drop of a grain of powder, Cummings will quote Article Two of the Bill of Rights, which states that "a well-regulated militia being necessary to the security of a free state, the right of the people to keep and bear arms shall not be infringed."

But Cummings's most novel contribution to the "right-to-bear-arms" controversy is a proposal for compulsory gun ownership in the United States, because "armed civilians are the measure of a democracy's strength." He admires Switzerland, where every man up to the age of fifty must keep either a loaded rifle or pistol in his home and attend annual target practice.

"You don't have much armed robbery with every home armed to the teeth," says Cummings. He argues that if guns were illegal, the honest man would be disarmed but the criminals and the lunatic fringe would continue to find contraband arms. He believes that the deranged student in the Texas tower would have done far less damage if swift answering fire had made him take cover, and that Lee Harvey Oswald, had he been unable to buy a cheap Italian carbine, would have tried to kill President Kennedy "with a Cossack saber."

Cummings is as abstemious as a seminarian—he neither smokes nor drinks, and the strongest word that passes his lips is "Gosh." He is also frugal, confessing to a Puritan streak. The apartments he keeps up in Washington, London, and Monaco are mainly

for business purposes. His Swiss chalet is comfortable but un-
pretentious.

He drives an old Opel station wagon, whereas the head of
his London office owns a fleet of six sports cars. Mentioning a
friend who came to see him in Monaco aboard his private yacht
with a crew of fourteen, Cummings says with a grimace, "You
become a slave to that." His only self-indulgences are good food
and a collection of 1,000 antique weapons, including early
flintlocks and wheel locks that would fetch up to $30,000 apiece
in today's gun market.

Early last August, Cummings was sipping ginger ale on the
flagstone terrace of his Swiss chalet, perched in the clean Alpine
air near the lake of Geneva 3,600 feet above sea level. Above,
a plane towed a red glider across a cloudless sky. Cummings was
reading over his July sales figures, and expressed surprise that,
despite the Negro riots, there had been no increase in his United
States sales. "You'd think our business would be a barometer for
that kind of thing," he said. "But it's the quiet time of year, before the hunting season opens."

After fifteen highly successful years in the gun business,
Cummings is quieting down himself. Since the Kennedy tax
reforms affecting Americans who live abroad, Monaco is no
longer a tax haven, but "just another nice place to live." Cummings is in the 80 percent bracket, and swears he'd be "better
off staring at the mountains than working."

Perhaps for that reason, or perhaps because he is mellow-
ing into a moralist, Cummings has dropped the hard sell in favor
of a philosophical, even fatherly, attitude toward his clients. On
occasion, he does his best to lose a sale. As he recently explained
to a Southeast Asian strongman: "Now look, you don't really
need 1,000 tanks. You have no aggressive plans. Your name
isn't Erwin Rommel. Keep your rice crop to feed your starving
peasants."